THE FORCE

by Stuart Wilde

"Understanding the Universal Law allows you to 'bend' reality and eventually knowledge sets you free."

THE FORCE

CONTENTS

Library of Congress Card Number 88-208213

International Standard Book Number ISBN 0-930603-00-1

First published in 1984
Sixteenth Printing May 1991
Seventeenth Printing March 1993

This book is published in Australia under license by
NACSON & SONS PTY LTD
P.O. BOX 515, BRIGHTON-LE-SANDS NSW 2216
PH: (02) 281 6179 ◆ FAX: (02) 281 2075

WHITE DOVE INTERNATIONAL, INC.
P.O. BOX 1000, TAOS NM 87571 USA
PHONE (505) 758-0500 ◆ FAX 505-758-2265

Airbrush cover by Rob Wood, Stansbury,
Ronsaville and Wood, inc. Annapolis, Maryland USA

CHAPTER 1: Reincarnation, Guides, and the Higher Self

At your birth, the spirit that is the *real* you entered the earth plane for a short period of special training. It chose the experience as part of a wider spiritual goal, for it knew there was no way it could reach that goal without first passing through the physical. Before you began your life, you knew what that spiritual goal was, and you had the ability to review (in a dimension beyond the earth plane) the general circumstances of your upcoming existence: the body your spiritual energy would inhabit; the parentage that would help you to develop; the geographic area you would find yourself in; your inter-personal relationships; your karmic ties; and the evolution of the earth at the time you were about to enter it. You, or the spiritual part of you anyway, reviewed all this and made its choice deliberately.

To understand this concept more fully, let us discuss the *real* you, that spirit entity that existed before your current existence on the earth plane. Since there are no words in our language to describe that energy, we will call it your *Higher Self.* Although this term can be misleading, because your real spiritual identity is not higher than you, it is you, let us accept it for simplicity's sake so that we can move on.

Your *Higher Self* is a collective body of energy. It is vast and ageless; it is everything that you have ever been, stretching back to the edge of infinity. Within it is all the knowledge that you will ever need and through it you can experience a limitless understanding of yourself and the physical plane, as well as of the unseen dimensions that lie close at hand. Your *Higher Self* is sustained by an intrinsic energy that is even bigger than itself. This sustaining energy we will call the *Force* or the *Living Spirit*.

The *Force*, like your *Higher Self*, is an energy that experiences evolution. It is massive, exhilarating, magnanimous beyond description—perhaps, you might want to call it God. It is not stagnant, as some would have you believe, it is growing, dynamic, and has an inner drive or desire to become more of itself. To achieve this, it divides itself into more and more separate parts or definitions, and it does so because it knows that, by dividing and spreading out, it will have more power and, having more power, it will grow.

The Force is a part of each and every thing in the physical plane. This includes our planet, the stars and galaxies, and the physical universe, as it stretches out in space, beyond our perceptions. By its very nature, the Force is immortal and never-ending and, because it is the inner light or "livingness" within all things, we call it *universal*. The more life force a thing expresses, the more complicated or greater is the extent of the Force within it. Therefore, a small bird expresses more of the Force than does a rock, and a human being expresses still more than a bird. But everything has the Force within it and that is the key to an individual's understanding.

The spiritual energy of your *Higher Self* also has the Force within it, and it too wants to grow. It began its existence by individualizing itself from the Force and it realized that, like the Force, it could expand by dividing itself into more and more experiences. Among the things it has been are your past lives, but even before it entered your human body, it had various experiences that would help it adjust to the vibrational force of the physical plane. Up to this point, it might have had twenty thousand experiences, maybe more. It would have had experiences as energy and light, as electricity and sound, as lesser forms of existence, which allowed it gradually to adjust to the earth plane. For the *Higher Self* would not enter the university of the physical experience in a complex form, it would have to go through energy experiences much like a kindergarten. It is interesting to think that there is a spiritual evolution in all things, that in the sound of a pebble tumbling over a cliff, or within a flower there are countless dimensions of evolution, *Higher Selves,* experiencing, training, destined, perhaps, one day to be human.

Six hundred lifetimes ago, your *Higher Self* might have had an experience as a cow and, bit by bit, learned to adapt its energy to the physical plane. As it learned, it became more courageous. Finally, it felt itself ready to enter the human form and it did so because, humanity being the highest expression of the Force on the earth plane, this was a natural progression for it to make.

Now, its first lifetime as a human being was not in a position of great responsibility, such as the president of a multi-national company. It was in something simple: a tribal life on the land or a lifetime in which it could almost stand on the sidelines and observe the goings on. Interestingly enough, Mongoloids and the mentally deficient are two examples of *Higher Selves* entering the physical plane for the first time—their lives are often short, they are usually surrounded by help and love, and little is expected of them.

After completing its first lifetime, the spiritual part of you that divided from the *Higher Self* to enter into your body drifts back to its source, reviewing its experiences as it goes. This period, or dimension, between the physical plane and your energy's re-envelopment into the *Higher Self* is sometimes called the "spirit world." It too is a part of the Force's experience and it too is growing and expanding, as are the spiritual energies that find themselves in that dimension.

The spirit world consists of thought forms and energy from the Force that vitalizes it. The thought patterns that you project into the spirit world are what you will experience. If you die as a Moslem, you will see mosques and minarets, and the spirits evolving around you will be Moslems. You will have a feeling that the spirit world consists only of Moslems. By being dogmatic about your beliefs, you see only what you believe in, and so the spirit world has a nice way of making everybody right.

The nature of that world is such that your thoughts and feelings are instantly magnified around you. Therefore, if you enter the spirit world in turmoil, you experience a heightened form of that thought pattern and an observer would say, subjectively, that you are in hell. Conversely, if your life is in balance at the time you separate from the physical body, you enter a spirit world of peace, harmony, and great beauty, and an observer would say, subjectively, that you are in heaven.

It is the nature of the vibrancy of the spirit world that has led to stories of heaven and hell being incorporated into the belief patterns of many religions.

When you enter the spirit world, your external experiences are in fact manifestations of the *inner you,* and it is this externalization that has become known in the holy books as the "last judgment." It is not a judgment in the sense that there is really any right or wrong. It is a judgment whereby you experience *yourself,* and in so doing you automatically drift to that area in the spirit world that is para-sympathetic with your energy pattern. Because you are aware not only of your own thoughts and feelings, but of the thoughts and feelings of others, they in turn perceive what it is that you really are. Each feeling that is a part of your *inner self* makes itself instantly manifest to you, and it becomes uncomfortable and totally disjointed for you to attempt to inhabit a part of the spirit world that is not similar to your energy.

On the earth plane, thoughts and feelings come back to you more slowly, and what makes the physical plane such a fascinating training ground is the fact that you practice controlling energy and its reactions without having to experience the consequences immediately. This allows you time to adjust before you go into higher planes of existence where energy patterns materialize faster and are thus harder to master.

This time lapse in the physical plane creates the illusion that the events in your life are controlled by some external force, be it God, or luck, or whatever, rather than by your own thought forms. Because the energy moves so slowly, it seems as if, it is not you who are creating your reality. You might indulge in a series of negative thoughts that will take two years to become manifest in your life, and you will say, "God did it to me." But once you raise your energy, you come into spiritual alignment with a higher evolutionary pattern, and find thought forms and feelings manifest almost instantly in front of you. It is as if, while still here on earth, you enjoy the exhilaration of another dimension, and understand it is *you* who create the events you experience, and your daily life is a reflection of what you actually are on an inner level.

This reflection continues in the spirit world. Consequently, evolution is not a matter of life before death and something different after death. It is eternal. The greater your expression of the Force on earth, the greater your experience in the afterlife. When you enter the spirit world, your energy will accentuate and you will experience an expansion of your inner self. If the opposite is the case, your energy will have a tendency to become less or lower, and this is why hell is described as a "going down," which, of course, it is if that is what you believe. In effect, hell is just one dimension alongside others, moving or oscillating with less vibrancy than those dimensions that express more of the Force.

It is important, therefore, not to be too concerned about life after death, but to create a strong expression of the Force before death. What you are right now is what you would experience in the spirit world, if you were to enter it today. Many people drift through life as if they had all the time in the world, and in a way they do, but the *Higher Self* went to great trouble to get them here, and at the slightest imbalance they may separate again. Life should be looked upon as an opportunity for growth, an incredible adventure, and no one should ever let a day pass without trying to expand his or her perceptions and personal expression of the Force.

After your first lifetime, your energy proceeded through the spirit world and finally reached back into itself, where it settled within your *Higher Self*. After a period of review, your *Higher Self* became restless to continue its evolution. An inner desire to continue its journey triggered the search for another life experience, and so it began to review its resources.

It knew what kind of life it needed if it was to continue its energy experience and, along with other *Higher Selves*, it waited and watched for a lifetime that suited its evolution and development.

Whenever two humans enter into a sexual relationship, the energy they create is read within the dimension of the *Higher Self*. That energy has a unique characteristic, much like a thumbprint, and when the *Higher Self* perceives a characteristic that fits its evolution, it moves forward, claiming that energy for itself. There is always one *Higher Self* that fits the pattern better than another, even though at times there may be more than one *Higher Self* that could accept a particular body. Sometimes, when identical twins are conceived, it becomes possible for two *Higher Selves* to enter into the earth plane at the same time, for similar experiences. But usually, twins who are physically identical have very different personalities because they have different *Higher Selves* and their evolutions are diverse.

When your *Higher Self* chooses a possible body (upon conception by the parents), it reviews in detail all the circumstances of the upcoming birth. It can see what physical weakness its future body might have and accepts it as part of its karmic evolution. For, within the *Higher Self*, disease is not a negative experience; it is a growth pattern to be relished for the greater understanding it provides.

Your *Higher Self* does not choose an incarnation on the earth plane on the basis of comfort or material status. It chooses an energy pattern that will help it to fill in the picture. Spiritual evolution is not a progression up a ladder. It is like fitting pieces into a jigsaw puzzle. In one experience you might choose the life of a recluse and, in the next, needing a more outward expression, you might choose a family of roving bandits. Even though a life like that might be a negative experience, it might allow your *Higher Self* a brief whirl of outward expression needed after a lifetime as a hermit.

To complete your evolution through it, you have to experience the earth plane in its totality. War, famine, and disease are all part of the karmic experience. Now, you might ask why the *Higher Self* would choose to enter a dimension of pain and suffering. The answer is that it is much like swimming a river; you cannot get to the other side without getting wet. Your *Higher Self* cannot come into an understanding of balance in the physical plane without suffering some of the bumps and bruises or rawness of life on earth. The physical is an immediate experience that creates an instant growth pattern within the *Higher Self*. It exposes you to great amounts of negativity; it is the university of "hard knocks." Realizations present themselves with rude abruptness and this allows the *Higher Self* to grow fast. Such is not generally the case in the spirit world. There, time does not exist and each evolutionary realization drifts gradually from within.

Some might say that the earth is harsh but, in its eternal sense, it is not, because negative experiences turn into positive learning when you view them in terms of your total evolution. This is why it is impossible to say that what others are going through is either good or bad: it is neither. Their lives are part of a pattern that they chose before they came here, or are patterns they have created while here, either through balance or through lack of it. Evolution is totally just. You experience whatever the *inner you* projects. Therefore, there are no accidents of birth, or quirks of fate, or misfortunes. All that you see around you is a lucid dream that you are experiencing for a short while in order to enhance your understanding. What makes it so exciting is that you can learn to change that dream to your own benefit, so that you experience only your highest growth and evolution.

But, no matter what your circumstances are, all was foreseen by the *Higher Self,* because within its cosmic overview it could perceive not only the body into which it would incarnate, but the general circumstances of its life on earth (for the first thirteen years anyway). It could see what type of relationship your parents were having and chose that balance or imbalance to work through its karmic patterns. It also knew where it would be geographically and this, along with your family's economic circumstances, make up a part of the evolution of your *Higher Self.* All the various patterns in your life, your homeland and its traditions and your family alignment, were part of your greater understanding and, no matter how difficult some of it may have been, it was all an element of the unfoldment of your *Higher Self,* as it strove to express even more of the Force. It knew what it was getting into and accepted it.

Your life's spiritual goal consists of experiencing and stepping above whatever circumstances you find yourself in. Anything that you find difficult or arduous is almost always your main karmic challenge. It is the aspect that you have to go beyond in order to complete your physical experience. And, in doing so, you have to begin wherever you find yourself, with whatever resources you have. It is pointless to wish that your body were stronger and your circumstances more fortunate because, if you need something different, your *Higher Self* would have chosen it.

It is by dealing with what you are, what you find in front of you, and by being responsible for your actions, that you go beyond the need to experience the challenge of negativity. Once you totally accept the fact that *you*, not fate, control your life, a door opens silently within you and, without your realizing it at first, you begin a higher evolution.

If negativity were not part of the curriculum, there would be no reason for the *Higher Self* to incarnate, because there would be no learning process.

For centuries philosopher's have struggled with the idea of a God who is supposedly good, yet seems to allow the suffering of mankind. This dichotomy has never been answered satisfactorily. Usually, you will be offered some lame response about God's plan, which is the philosophers' way of saying, "I don't know the answer."

In fact, pain and suffering are not part of God's plan. They are factors of the coarseness of the vibrational field of the physical plane. The Force is not involved. It does not even have an immediate awareness of the negativity. If it did, it would have to be it, and the Force cannot be a negative energy. Picture it like this: you are watching a film about the suffering of the starving millions and can perceive what they are going through. However, it is not a part of your destiny in this life to experience dying in the gutter. You are cognizant of the circumstances of the starving people because you are watching the film, but the whole event is outside the scope of your involvement, and there is nothing you can do about it without infringing on the people's right to experience whatever evolution they have chosen. It is the same for the Force. It can see and feel what is going on, but it is not a part of the pattern. It is an energy of indescribable power experiencing evolution outside the vibrational waveband of the negative experience. In the same way, when you watch the film, you are experiencing life beyond starvation.

It is by projecting your energy and experiencing its results that you come into an understanding of life and its energy patterns. In the course of a number of lifetimes, you balance what you are to the point where you finally understand the true nature of quest, and your position as custodian of the Force becomes obvious. When that occurs you have no further need to remain on the earth plane and you proceed naturally to other evolutions in other dimensions of existence.

If you think about it, the physical plane has a built-in governor: if a life experience is extremely harsh, the body deteriorates, the experience is over quickly, and the inner spiritual energy withdraws and returns to the *Higher Self.* This allows the physical plane to maintain a correct evolution and balance. Modern technology often holds an evolving spirit in a deteriorating body for years, even though, inwardly, the spirit is crying to get out, crying to return to its true self. That is also part of the learning process.

There is no shortcut to completing your earth experience. You will have to experience all of it for, metaphysically, you can only go beyond something by going through it. Your life builds upon a pattern and, eventually, that pattern sets you free. You may have experienced lifetimes of great poverty, or your *Higher Self* may have chosen to experience a body with physical restrictions, or perhaps you find yourself encased within the confines of social structures or strict religious surroundings, where deviation from the norm is impossible. All this is used by your *Higher Self* to experience growth and evolution.

It chooses restriction in order to experience a fast concentration of energy. Imagine it as a cloud large enough to cover an entire field. Suddenly the cloud decided to enter a tin can in the far left corner of the field. In order to do so, it would have to concentrate its energy, which would cause its energy to move faster. This would enable it to express more of the Force, and so it would grow. The same applies to you. The more you concentrate your energy, the faster it oscillates, and the more of the Force you express. As this happens, worlds and dimensions that are oscillating slightly faster than you are open to your perceptions.

This opening is the key to life and the reason for understanding the Force within you is so that you can, through your own efforts, graduate from the circumstances in which you find yourself. Anything that you can do to help yourself, helps your *Higher Self* to move toward its goal and, as it approaches that goal, you will feel the excitement of worlds that you did not know existed.

During your first six energy experiences or lifetimes, you have assigned to you two spiritual beings or karmic angels. These spiritual entities are evolving and they experience growth through the service they perform. The guardian angels are assigned to you to ensure that you complete the experience that you entered into and do not drift far from your target, which you might have a tendency to do. Remember, the *Higher Self* expressing as you is not accustomed to the restriction you are now experiencing, and its choice of a life on earth might be very challenging.

Let us say, for example, your fourth incarnation was as a woman, in a period when the role of women was very restricted. Your father married you off to a local tyrant, and you could not express yourself beyond the mundane chores of housekeeping and childbearing, and you brought forth eleven children. You might want to commit suicide, in order to escape the restrictions. The angels would express energy toward you, giving you a little inspiration beyond the difficulty of your situation, and that inspiration would hold you in the pattern long enough for you to complete the experience. This does not mean that the karmic angels control your destiny, far from it. They project energy, but what you do with it is up to you. Their role is to allow you to complete the totality of an experience.

At the end of these exploratory lifetimes—on average six—you will automatically gravitate to a lifetime that allows you greater freedom. As a man, you might choose the life of an explorer, or, as a woman, you might choose to be the only daughter of a rich landowner, from whom you would inherit a position of great responsibility. Ownership of the land would allow you economic stability and you would express yourself through the variety of possibilities that the position of landowner would afford.

After your first six lifetimes, you will be basically in the closing stages of the evolutionary experience of the earth plane, and incarnations will come more quickly. At this point, you will be joined by an even more powerful energy. This evolving energy, which we call your guide, having completed its lifetimes in the earth experience, has the perception and understanding to help you fulfill your life's goal.

Again, do not be put off by terms. What we refer to as the guide can be looked upon as an inspirational energy, a kind of spiritual intuition, that has your evolution at heart. If you allow your intellect to react too much, you can get bogged down in definitions and never really get a grip of the concept. Think of it like this: if you were in a dark cave and someone turned on a light, you would not care what the light was called, as long as you could see what you were doing. As mortals, we tend to want things defined in little boxes, and yet how do we define the undefinable?

The energy or guide that helps you with your life's goal is different for each of your lifetimes. Often it will be someone with whom you have been closely associated in a past life: your mother, a brother, a close friend or lover, an energy now beyond the earth plane that accepts the position of guide, in service to you and the Force. It does so as an expansion of its understanding. How well your guide performs is inexorably linked to how well you do. The more energy you are able to accept, the more it will push forward, and the more it pushes forward, the more you will evolve. But the guide has to wait for you.

It is important to realize that the guide does not have all the answers just because it is beyond the earth plane. It has to work with energy like the rest of us: nothing is predestined. Furthermore, if everything is not brought together correctly, the guide might find itself repeating the guiding process with other individuals until such time as it understands the correct projection of energy, balance, and imbalance.

And so, as you grow, the guide grows with you, gradually pulling more and more energy around you, the key being the level at which you are able to accept its power. Deep within you there lies a special creativity: it might be in the fine arts, or an ability with animals, or the capacity to be a great teacher, peacemaker, or diplomat, or anything else. These talents become encrusted with your limitations and never surface—trapped by fear, laziness, or spiritual ineptitude. If, however, you enliven yourself and begin to express your creativity, the guide will have something to work with and will pull in other guides and energies that have expertise in your field of interest. Suddenly, you have two, three, maybe more, guides helping you and, as this awakening of consciousness takes place, you might suddenly decide it is time to do something about the condition of your body. As you begin to work on that, your guide pulls in a healing energy that shows you what you need for optimum power, and you grow stronger still. The more you move toward the light, the more is added. And, as the process gathers speed, you will notice growth in your life in a matter of weeks.

Understanding the Force is understanding your *Higher Self.* Your guide is there but, more than anything else, the growth process is a clearing away of the debris of old thought patterns, bad habits, sloppy performances, and gummy thinking. If everything that you are is clogged by negativism, judgment, and body imbalance, you cannot be a channel for energy. The Universe is ready and waiting to enhance your development for, as you develop, so does the totality of the Force develop. By expanding your consciousness, you help everyone else to expand, because, first, we all have the Force within us, and, second, when people perceive the growth in you they begin to look at themselves, and each will raise the energy of the other.

Nothing in the Universe is controlled or guaranteed. Your guide does not control your destiny or decide what you are going to have for breakfast. It projects energy allowing an opening, a new perspective. You may be walking down a road you have traveled a dozen times and suddenly you will see a group of trees that you never knew was there. That is the guide teaching through your *Higher Self*. It is fascinating to think that everything in the Universe is around you right now, every dimension, every invisible spirit, every higher inspiration. It is a matter of controlling the physical, emotional, and mental cacophony that dominates daily life and then, suddenly, "click," a gate swings gently on its hinges and before you lies another world—a world that has been there since the beginning, a world of initiates, a world open to all but attained by few. The Force within you is the key. By recognizing it and understanding the interaction between you and your *Higher Self*, you begin to control your own destiny. For you cannot go beyond the earth plane until you accept that *you*, not fate, create the events in your life: that your experiences, pleasant or unpleasant, are but outer manifestations of the *inner you*. Once you accept those facts unequivocably, you rise beyond mass thinking, discarding the constraints of "accepted limitations" in the way that you might throw out an old shoe.

But to go beyond the world is hard. You will constantly face your *inner self*, its uncertainties, its illusions, its challenges. Bit by bit, you peel away the various layers, eventually reaching a complete communication with your *Higher Self*, and all the power and knowledge that is stored there is available to you. You will find yourself able to use information you never knew was there. As this energy flows, its exhilaration will carry you from stepping stone to stepping stone and you will find life magically unfolding in front of you. You will turn and look back, and wonder what took you so long.

CHAPTER 2: Understanding the Force

The Force is universal, which means that it is in everything. It is also endless: it stretches out not only to an eternity behind you, but infinitely into the future. The Force is also all knowing because, being in all things, it knows from its own experience.

Your life's goal is to expand the Force within you so that you can perceive beyond what you are now. First, you have to recognize that the Force *is* within you. Next, you have to acknowledge yourself as God, as part of the Living Spirit within. No matter what you are physically, what imbalances you might suffer, what situations you have created, you are still a part of the Force. If you recognize that and accept your intrinsic goodness or holiness, then the Force within you will magnify because you are concentrating on it, and you accept being a part of it.

You might like to start the day with a personal affirmation, saying: "I am the Force within. What I am is eternal, immortal, universal, and infinite. What I am has beauty and strength. This day is my day, and all that I pull to me is for my highest evolution and growth." Do this early in the morning and the power of the Force increases. It acts as your protector as you step into the day. By recognizing the Force and not compromising your position, you enter a special energy that allows light to flow from within you, out to the people you deal with. This energy begins to be felt by others and, like a hippopotamus rising languorously from its hippopotamus dreams, an immense power stirs, and all sit up and take notice.

When you have enough of the Force within you, you are ready to move out from your inner being. You can accept new associations and positions with confidence and, as you take total responsibility for yourself, people will feel the energy and they will ask you to take responsibility for their projects and so on. You can never be unemployed, because most people shun responsibility as if it were an exotic disease!

Once you have recognized that the Force is within you, and that *you*, not fate, God, or anyone else, control your life, you are ready for the next step, which is basically familiarizing yourself with your *Higher Self* and its flow of energy in your life. Much like presenting yourself at some royal court, you have to learn the formalities and characteristics of the energy pattern, what it responds to and best expresses in your life. This part of your training can be exhilarating, for daily life becomes a symbol of your progress and you pass nothing without seeing its inner message. This dialogue manifests in a symbolic unfolding, and the tramp on the corner who spoke to you on the way to the station is no longer a tramp, but a symbol, a single word in a cosmic paragraph, teaching you about yourself.

As you learn to view the world as your teacher, you find that your *Higher Self* leads you gently back into yourself. It is said that when the student is ready, the teacher will appear. But you have to begin to move toward what it is you want, making use of what you have right now. Otherwise, ineptitude rivets your expectations to the floor. Everything around you is there to help you go to the next step, but there is no automatic graduation. You cannot mumble mystery words, cavort over a mystic symbol at midnight and say, "I am the initiate," and expect the Force to respond—it will not. But by moving toward it and accepting responsibility for your life, you complete the next step.

To understand the projections of the Force, you have to understand the subconscious mind, which is like a large map on which are recorded the past events of your life. Your waking reality is but a torchlight shining onto one small section of the map. You can see just the events around you; the rest of the map is still there but to you it lies in darkness, and so is beyond your conscious perception.

In a hypnotic trance you could review everything you have ever done, every word you have spoken, every experience you have been through—it is all there. You could recall how many footsteps it took to get to work today, or you could recall your first coherent words. Nothing is lost, for within the mind are stored billions upon billions of units of information, and these pieces of information or characteristics make up the *inner you*.

This system of recording begins at birth. The mind programs and stores all your thoughts and feelings, and it accepts whatever emotions, fears, and limitations it is taught. If a mother says to her child, "Put on your coat or you'll catch your death of cold," the subconscious mind of the child accepts that as an authoritarian belief pattern, and the next time the child goes out without a coat, his or her mind brings forward that energy and says, "lack of coat: sickness," and he or she develops a cold.

This type of negative programming builds up, and for the first thirteen years of life children accept totally whatever their parents or guardians tell them.

They accept their elders' beliefs, attitudes, values, and thought patterns. After their thirteenth year, they spiritually come of age and begin to experience and develop the energy that has been created. What unfolds in their teen years is often uncomfortable, as they try to bring their belief patterns into a coherent identity of self.

The process of dealing with the mind, its negativities, its emotions, feelings, and attitudes, is the key to spiritual growth. Each thought and feeling that you have about yourself is expressed on an inner plane as energy, and that energy, interacting with the Universal Law, creates the events and circumstances of your life. You can watch this inner energy by watching what is around you. Do you have nothing but beauty and a richness of life? Or are there areas that you would like to improve? By looking at your *inner self* you grow and, in doing so, you expand the level of the Force you express.

As was said, the Force is a totally positive energy. It cannot be a part of negativity, for its evolution is beyond that. If you stand in an alley with a big stick in your hand and you brain and rob the first unfortunate who happens along, the Force is not a part of that act. The Force is in the stick, in the blood, and in the wallet you stole, but it is not responsible for the event, nor does it experience the event as negativity. It has no emotion, it is just a divine energy, an observer, not a participant; it evolves in a dimension of perception beyond the physical and is yet a part of it.

The more you train your mind and feelings to emphasize the positive, the more you become like the Force, a divine observer, not connected emotionally with the frailties of human life. However, more is involved than just taking a positive attitude to life. You have to begin to look at whatever limitations lie in the *inner you*, for the Force is unlimited, and the less restricted you become the more of the Force you will express. Every time you turn and face yourself and look at your reactions and feelings, you basically clean away another small particle of debris that has accumulated.

In the legend of the Holy Grail, this facing of one's inner uncertainties is symbolized by the slaying of the dragon. In overcoming limitation, you move closer to the next dimension—a dimension of unparalleled exhilaration, existing beyond day-to-day perceptions. In actuality, you begin to leave the earth plane, for, even though your body might still be here, your inner energy is moving away from the physical. This creates an island of strength and beauty all around you, and from that island you, as the quiet observer, look back at the world. You become the same as the Force in the stick the robber used in the alley, not reacting to the emotions of others, living your own creation, a world apart.

Ah! but what about helping others, you might ask. If you go deep within yourself and clear out the negativity there, you begin to raise your energy. As you do so, you will help others, not because you have assisted them materially, but because you have raised your consciousness. This might sound obscure, but it is a cosmic fact that first you have to heal yourself, you have to find the grail before you will ever be much use to others. You can send them a bag of rice, if you wish, but that will not increase, by one iota, their expression of the Force. To really help people, you have to show them how to increase their power, and if you have not completed your own journey, what will you show them? Confusion? Once you have raised your energy, people will be pulled to you automatically. You will not have to go out and say, "Come here, I'll heal you." People will come to you, because those who are growing spiritually seek examples of the Force, which is moving faster than they are, for such examples enhance their own expression of beauty by causing their energy to move faster.

As you develop, your perceptions become more acute. You experience extrasensory powers, or clairvoyance or clairaudience, or, more likely, clairsentiousness (a heightened sense of feeling), and you find yourself in places and situations where you just *know* what is going to happen next. This power of perception is very strong, it may be tempting to impress others with your new-found prowess and, before you know it, you have set up your "Madame Zora" gypsy booth and are advising others.

This is fine as long as you realize that psychic power can be a trap. Real metaphysical perception lies in the power of silence. The more you interact with the ordinary world, the more that world holds you in the physical. Beyond the "psychic" is another dimension, but many people, hooked by the glamour or kudos of having a power a little beyond ordinary, never reach it.

If you stay in the world of psychic perception too long, you will miss the boat metaphysically, and you will not reach that dimension of the Force from which a demonstration of psychic ability is seen as nothing more important than a small child banging two bricks in a playpen. By developing silently, you hold a power to yourself, and the more you do so, the more doors open ahead of you, but you have to travel through the silence, perhaps for many years, and you have to trust that there will be more up ahead. Many modern psychics accept a few fleeting impressions as the totality of their ability and, by constantly presenting their energy to others, burn themselves out on an inner level. They then have no momentum to carry themselves across to other planes, and eventually this misuse is apt to become manifest as disease. Next time you visit a psychic or medium who has been involved for many years, look at his or her body before you decide if the life of a psychic reader is worth it. A high percentage of them are totally worn out.

I mention this because people get trapped in the stupidities of the ego. As you move toward the Force, you will find that the ego begins to die and the subconscious moves over to allow the *real* you to control your life. Of course, the ego does not give up without a fight! When you consider that you have been putting energy into the subconscious for years, you will realize that it is going to take effort and discipline to stop doing so. There will be setbacks and "dark nights of the soul," when it seems that you face the insurmountable, but that is just the energy of the subconscious mind rebelling, refusing to give up its dominant position. It will use every trick in the book because, as you express more and more of the Force, your mind will gradually lose its grip and for a time you might even feel that you are dying.

That is why stories of the initiates such as Lazarus involve dying and rising again. When those stories were written there were no words to describe psychological, metaphysical, *inner* events. Therefore, the writers said that Lazarus died and came back to life through his contact with metaphysical understanding (which in his case was represented by the Nazarene).

Similarly, the initiates of the Great Pyramid were placed in a sarcophagus or tomb, and there they would symbolically die. Using herbs and various mind-control techniques, the High Priest would assist the student to experience an inner vision of dimensions beyond the earth plane. In order for this to happen successfully, the student had to enter a catatonic trance, centering his subconscious mind enough to perceive beyond the physical. The writers of that time, not totally comprehending what was going on, wrote to the limits of their understanding. And so you will find that the story of the initiate entering the tomb or sarcophagus, dying and rising again after three days, pervades many religions and cults. Some, such as the Egyptian mysteries and cult of Mythra, were common knowledge before the time of the Nazarene.

Jewish writers knew of the mysteries of the Great Pyramid because the Jewish tribes had spent many years in Egypt, and the cult of Mythra was the religion of the Roman occupiers of the Holy Land. And so you will find that the stories of the Nazarene follow closely the stories of Mythra and the ancient Egyptian traditions.

At the end of the three-day period, the student understood his true cosmic reality, and it was said he came back to life to return to the world as an initiate, pledged to a vow of secrecy. In effect, as the negativity of the mind loses predominance over your day-to-day affairs, what you think you are dies, and gradually the *real* you comes to life. As the energy of your *Higher Self* begins to establish a stronger pattern, you literally become the initiate, but the process is gradual, a tussle between inner objectives.

To win this battle is your prime spiritual objective. By centering and disciplining your subconscious mind, you allow the energy of the Force to flow. At first, you will feel that the Force is not there, for its power, expressed through your *Higher Self*, is not a power you will ever be able to touch, taste, hear, or see. You may have a fleeting impression of its being with you and you will see it working in your life, but you will not be able to experience it directly. It comes round the subconscious mind like a wind. You will know that something is happening, but you will not be sure what. As you gradually raise your energy you will know it is there because of an exhilaration of self, but you will never have concrete proof. You will just notice if it ever leaves or drops.

Once established, this constant flow from the *Higher Self* becomes addictive. In fact, you will become frightened at not being a part of it, for you will find yourself abandoned in the world, with all its uncertainties and fears. By keeping up your energy, however, allowing nothing to impinge upon your expression of life, and knowing and working with the power daily, you actually build around you an invisible energy curtain. This power is moving faster than the energy you meet in daily life, and so negativity projected to you bounces off and you have a shield of total power.

This expression of positive power goes out ahead of you. As you walk up to it in your day, all is balanced and in flow, and you are immediately aware of any pitfalls, for there are no accidents in life, no innocent victims. Through a balance or a lack of balance, you control every event in your life. The man in the alley who is struck by a stick is involved deeply on an inner level, because his energy, his imbalance, his thought forms, brought him to where he found himself in the alley being robbed. If he had had more of the Force within him, he would have turned left not right, and we would find him half a mile away in a shop eating cake, and the energy pattern of the robbery would be a part of anothers person's growth and evolution.

Ah! But ... what if? What if the man in the alley had been delayed, what if ... ? Within the power of the Force, there are no "what ifs." It is you, only you, who create every moment of your life. Whatever you experience is of your own making. If you want to make progress spiritually, you have to accept that fact. You are living in a dangerous world; at any minute you may be plucked out. You have a responsibility to maintain balance in your thoughts, in your emotions and feelings, in your physical body. If you do not, you will find yourself in an energy pattern that is out of control. It may manifest as something small, like an argument at work, or as something more threatening: some loony jumps the traffic light in front of you and pins your car to the side of the bus station, and your energy departs for the spirit world. People say, "Poor Harry, such an unfortunate accident, it must have been the will of God."

But it is not the will of God, and you should not give the Force a bad name, because it is not involved. It is Harry's energy, what he felt about his life, his lack of power, the argument he had with his wife just before he left, the two whiskeys too many the night before, the lack of respect he felt for his body, the energy he built over the years, the way he expressed that energy in his life; all these things led him to that traffic light at that particular moment to experience a growth pattern. When Harry gets back to his *Higher Self*, he will understand how his life was his responsibility. He will see it all, not in pain and anguish, but as a learning. For within the *Higher Self*, all is alkaline and positive—there is no sin.

There is nothing you can do that can be regarded metaphysically as sinful. There is high energy that expresses the Force and there is less high energy, but that is all. Whatever you create, you experience. Its effects will be around you when you die, as they are while you are alive, and your life is a matter of learning to deal with that. A person who violates the rights of others infringes on their freedoms and creates an energy of restriction around himself: that, in turn, pulls to him others who will violate his rights. It is not crime and punishment in the sense of retribution for sin, it is more energy in motion, its consequence, if you like.

Sin is a creation of the subconscious mind. It is a moral code based on various tribal customs, and contravention of that code is regarded by tribal members as sinful. However, what is sinful to you is not sinful to someone else. In Africa, high on the plains of the Serengeti, there is a small tribal village that has been there many years. Every morning, the men of the village rise and walk casually to the end of the village, where they urinate up against a particular tree (God knows what it does for the tree!). This is accepted behavior and the women of the village do not react to it. Now, take a few friends, go to the local bus stop tomorrow around eight o'clock in the morning, and do the same thing; then write to me from prison and let me know how your "villagers" reacted. Sins are a creation of the mind, a shifting sea of customs, rules, and traditions.

The laws of the Force are beyond emotion. Because the Force is just energy, it does not make judgments about your performance. It is perfect love, neutral. It has certain symmetric patterns that seem to unfold according to whatever energy you put in, but these patterns do not stand in judgment against you. They just unfold according to the level of balance you maintain.

So it is in physical evolution that you practice understanding the Force; learning to work with balance and control, in conditions suited to you, until such time as you are ready to leave for higher ground. When that happens, you are joined by the guiding energy that will help you evolve more quickly. That guiding power is with you right now, as you read this book, ensuring that you have what you need for your growth.

Let us review: To understand the Force, you have to acknowledge its existence. Then you have to recognize that, since it is in all things and in you, you have the power to control all things. By controlling your mind, you can perceive all things. Discipline sets you free to project the Force to your own ends, and those ends will lead you gradually into evolutions beyond where you are now. And that is important.

CHAPTER 3: Developing a Flow of
Communication with the Force

Once you understand that the Force is in all things and that you can use it to your benefit, you then need a working knowledge of how it manifests and what levels of energy are available to you.

Let us discuss more fully your guide and how its evolution is linked to yours. Often the term *spirit guide* conjures up visions of a Victorian seance, with a white-haired old lady squeakily asking the ceiling, "Is anybody there?" This image of guides confuses. The guide is not an Egyptian prince, or a Red Indian chief, or a nun from the Renaissance. It is an energy evolving beyond the reincarnational pattern of the physical plane, and because its energy is slightly beyond your perception, your subconscious mind creates a symbol it understands, and brings forward an image of a Red Indian because that feels comfortable to it. Then the energy has to have a name, and so the mind creates one, and so on, a process of the subconscious mind creating images it understands.

If you were walking through a wood and saw a nature spirit, your mind would not understand the energy pattern, because the nature spirit's energy would be a flashing, vibrant life force, moving faster than the eye can normally perceive, indefinable to the subconscious mind. But your mind, not liking to accept a visual pattern with which it is not familiar, automatically reorganizes the information into a symbol that it understands, and you will say: "I saw this little leprechaun wearing a green hat and sitting on a rock. It was playing a flute." That is the peculiarity of the mind and its symbols.

Your guide is also a spontaneous flash of vibrant life force using its vibrancy to help you evolve. And because of your guide's position, associated as it is with your *Higher Self*, it acts as a key, allowing you a storehouse of perception. This information is vital to your growth, but it will not come forward until you are ready to accept it on an energy level. For your guide is not going to blow you away, by overloading the circuit. It has more power than you will ever need, but a part of your guide's learning is to collate all that power, omitting nothing, then ply it out to you in quantities that will not put you into imbalance.

I once attended a mind-control course in London, England. One of the students was a simple lad with an endearing genuineness about him. The course lasted over two consecutive weekends, during which time he had a great spiritual awakening. He learned about the mind, the hidden capacities of man, the Ancient Wisdoms, and he became inspired. No doubt his guide was pleased and pushed forward even more energy. A crescendo began to build in the young man. He touched his inner power strongly and quickly, and soon began to feel himself invincible. He felt himself the greatest spiritual being on the earth plane.

Now, his subconscious mind had a symbol in it that said, "Jesus of Nazareth was the highest spiritual being that ever lived." Therefore, the lad felt that he must be Jesus. Two weeks later, he attended a "follow-up" workshop lecture. On entering the meeting room, he declared that he was Jesus and that his energy was invincible. The others stood around mumbling "heah, heah!" and taking little notice. Whereupon, the young man, feeling a need to demonstrate the great power he felt from within, announced that he could fly. Still he was ignored. Moments later, much to the consternation of all present, he launched himself from the second story of the building into a fountain in the courtyard below. Interestingly enough, the janitor of the building, having decided that very day that it was time for the fountain's annual cleaning, had emptied it! Our young "questor" flew through the air from forty feet and found himself in the arms of solid concrete.

His guide resigned!

I offer this story to demonstrate that, in dealing with energy, it is possible to become overloaded. The guide has to ensure that you maintain a cohesive balance to your evolution, he has to make power available to you, but the limit is you.

The key, therefore, is how much you can open to the Force, that benevolent power that has been waiting for you since the beginning of time. Many wish to be great communicators, to channel a higher energy in the New Age, and yet they do not understand that energy can flow only in quantities they are ready to accept. A simple rule, but many miss the point.

If you want to teach, bring a power, a healing for the New Age—begin with yourself, begin by looking at the energy of your life. See what is holding you back; old associations, negative ways, poor eating habits, a lack of purpose, a lack of courage perhaps. Taking stock of your position will probably make you realize you have everything you need and that your life's goal lies in front of you: if it did not, you would have left the earth plane some time ago and would be experiencing evolution elsewhere.

Communicating with your guide and your *Higher Self* is mostly a matter of discipline. You have to go at it as if your life depended on it. Your mind is strong. It has been in command for many years and will not give ground unless it has to. The effort is like swimming against the current, and, as you clear away the debris, the light shines ever stronger and its power encourages you to go deeper.

But first you must rouse what you think you are. Your mind has created many rigid patterns—habits, if you will—and it will hold to these habits as if its life depended on them, which in a way it does. Shake the tree! Break the routines. Allow constant change to create freshness around you. Get up at three o'clock in the morning and have breakfast then, just as your mind protests, surprise it, take it to an icy lake and throw it in.

By radically altering the patterns around you, you confuse your mind into releasing its grip, and that is your key to a fuller experience of the higher powers. Right now, the power of your mind, your emotions, what you believe about yourself, create an impenetrable barrier through which the Force cannot flow. Once you have disciplined your mind and controlled your emotions, the energy of your *Higher Self* will flow through, and the more it does, the more light you will have for your path; trouble will melt away and you will fully understand what was meant by "the Golden Age."

Without discipline, your chances are slim: in truth, they are nil.

CHAPTER 4: The Four Disciplines of the Initiates

Mention discipline to your subconscious mind and it will reach for its hat and coat!

Why?

Because your mind knows that when you establish discipline it will lose control, and it will not give ground unless it absolutely has to.

To win the battle, you have to create as high an energy as possible, then guard it, watching carefully to keep it up at all times. As long as your energy is high, you will control, but let it drop and your subconscious will dominate. The very nature of the physical plane will conspire to pull you down, partly because of its baseness, and partly because you will become tired, or your eating habits will be poor, or you will let negative emotions creep into your life. Your evolutionary learning process is dominated by your ability to recognize and control the ebb and flow of energy around you. For, like all energy, metaphysical energy is volatile and never stays still: if it is not going up, it is going down.

Even though you will never have a concrete experience of the Force, your inner feelings will tell you when it is with you and when it is not, and soon you will train yourself to recognize the subtleties of energy affecting your life.

The four personal disciplines, which were known in the olden days as the Four Disciplines of the Initiates, are:

Physical Discipline
Nutritional Discipline
Emotional Discipline
The Discipline of Balance

Each one warrants a book unto itself, but a brief discussion of them here, will give you the groundwork, and you will be able to handle the rest for yourself.

Physical discipline is acquired through a knowledge of your body. When you have a thorough understanding of your physical experience, you will step above it and a gate will open automatically. It is impossible to have a higher experience until you have mastered the one you are in. This does not mean that you have to heal your every ailment instantly. What the discipline asks is that you take responsibility for your body, learn about it, practice controlling it, exercise it, and respect it, making sure that the physical experience does not become a runaway horse and cart to the point where your body controls you, rather than you control it. If there is disease in your body, do not roll over and quit. Instead, you should affirm: "What I am is the Force within, I am not my body, I am not my emotions, I am not my mind; I am eternal, immortal, and infinite, and what I am has beauty and strength, and there is nothing I cannot learn to control."

There are various ways of learning about your body and establishing control: Yoga, exercise, meditation, sitting still, taking walks in silence, fasting and cleansings, and study. Choose whatever path you wish but choose one, for it is important for you to know what you are doing.

Just for fun, put down this book and place your finger *exactly* on your pancreas. If you are not sure where your pancreas is, put your finger where you think it is. Then get a book on human anatomy and you will probably laugh, because a great percentage of those asked have no idea where their pancreas is or what is its function. One lady in a recent seminar placed her finger behind her right ear! (Just for the record, the pancreas is under the stomach and it runs crossways from the duodenum to the spleen.)

This exercise is important because it illustrates that most people know little about the bodies they are in. Consequently, when something goes wrong, their minds react in fear, fueled by ignorance. Each pain becomes a trauma, rather than a signal for them to commence the appropriate self-healing. Once you know how your body works, what vitamins and minerals it needs, and how its various components function, you are able to establish around you a confident power. This power allows you to feel that you, not doctors, or drugs, or some outside force, control your body, that you have the power to heal whatever circumstance might develop and that you can live without fear. Once you have established that fact, you can turn your mind to other things. But it is difficult to effect total control if you think your pancreas is behind your ear.

Take time to understand yourself physiologically; your digestion, duodenum, pancreas, colon, gall bladder, liver, kidney. How do the various functions of your body work? How does your blood flow? How is energy carried through your nervous system? What constitutes healthy teeth, hair, gums, eyes, and so on? Once you understand the nature of your vehicle, you are in a position to dominate it.

Next, establish a firm understanding that you are

not your body, that you *are* the energy of your *Higher Self*, a part of the God Force. You are in this body because you *chose* it, and what it has become is not the will of God. It is what you have created with your thought patterns and experiences so far. There is nothing you cannot reverse—but people sometimes find themselves trapped by habit. You can inspire someone to give up salt and they might cut down to just six bags of salty potato chips per day, then wonder why the universe is punishing them when things fall apart—that is the way of ordinary people.

The path demands a special dedication. It demands that you impose absolute control, for as you raise your energy the path gets narrower: the slightest slip and you may plunge from a great height. There are no grey areas. Either you are in control or you are not, and the Force, being totally impartial, cares not one way or the other. The history of man is full of stories of individuals who felt that God or something was going to save them at the last minute. Where are they? They are in the next dimension, understanding differently.

If you want to be more than you are now, you have to take to the task in a full frontal attack. This attitude of self-determination is known as "The Path of Power," or "The Way of the Warrior." Emotive terms perhaps, but you need power to break through the constraints of your mind, and control of the physical is the first step of your journey.

Once you have this control, you automatically enter an exclusive dimension, for the outside world knows little about balance and so your energy becomes a part of the Universe where the power of the Force is felt, and that will attract others. Most people live bland lives; they are like jellyfish plopped in a puddle, they are not going anywhere and eventually the puddle evaporates and they depart the physical. By controlling your body, you hoist your jellyfish out of the puddle into a pond and from there out into the ocean, which in this case is the energy expression of the Force.

The next discipline, nutritional discipline, is closely linked to the first. For you will have to express whatever you are to become through your body, and that body will have to eat. There is no faster way of raising your energy than adopting good eating habits. Foods such as salt, sugar, and refined products have a tendency to lower energy, whereas such foods as fruit and vegetables raise it. As you center on controlling the physical, your body's nutritional needs become clear and you gradually become your own healer.

But the healing process cannot occur unless you maintain an alkaline balance in the food you eat. If your diet is too acid, or if you eat excessive amounts of food, your body never gets a chance to rebuild and heal itself. Consequently, it gradually deteriorates. Proteins, alcohol, nuts, grains, and dairy products (except yogurt) along with sugar and salt are acid foods. Fruits, vegetables and juices are alkaline. For optimum balance, you need an 80 percent alkaline diet. This means concentrating on fruits and raw vegetables, using proteins only in small quantities, for when you need energy. A person in control of his life needs only about 50 grams of protein a day. This should consist of just 7 ounces of flesh protein or a vegetarian equivalent or 36 ounces of yogurt, depending on the brand. The rest of your diet should be alkaline.

There are some exceptions. For example, if you are in a very strenuous or physical occupation, you may need more than 50 grams of protein a day. There are many books to help you learn about nutrition, and the more you know the more you control. Generally speaking, people eat far too much acid, and that creates a hotbed for disease.

Unfortunately, there are almost no packaged, bottled, or canned goods that do not contain either sugar or salt. Sugar is used to appeal to your emotions. Salt is used as a preservative and continues to act as such after ingestion. Food so treated tends to linger in your body, not digesting correctly, putrefying, and eventually causing disease. You may find it necessary to give up buying that kind of food, and to rely mostly on fruits, vegetables, grains, and unpackaged goods. Preparing such foods takes a little more effort but you have to make the choice. Each instant of your life, you make decisions that affect your development, and the combination of those decisions shows up in the circumstances you experience. What you eat creates your body. The more you rely on fresh foods that have the life force in them, the more energy you will have. There is little life force in pizza: sad but true.

In conclusion, it is best for you to maintain an alkaline diet, avoid sugar and salt, and, as long as you do not abuse it with alcohol, cigarettes, or drugs, your body will heal itself, and, as your energy rises, your aches and pains will fall away. It takes time. Often, poor condition results from tens of thousands of unbalanced meals and this is not reversed in one day. You have to be patient with yourself.

Once you are on the path, have learned about your body, and accepted responsibility for it, you are ready for the third discipline, emotional discipline. This follows automatically. As you work on your body and your nutrition and begin to move away from the coarseness of the physical, your mind will react emotionally, and mental discipline is the hardest of all.

You think you have your energy under control, then suddenly an upset occurs and it all falls apart.

This is because the mind has an attitude. It thinks events and circumstances are real and acts accordingly. When your energy drops your mind becomes capricious and argumentative, making unreasonable demands. What happens on an energy level is that the orange, or emotional, part of your aura, spikes into the red (the physical) and the yellow (the mental) on either side of it. Your body reacts physically and your mind reacts with frenzy, and you find yourself bickering with the world and yourself.

The key to establishing control is to spend a part of each day completely alone. Use the time to review your feelings and concerns—allow an emotional maturity to develop whereby you deeply understand that nothing is real, that there is no death, that all is evolution. This will detach you from the emotional impetus of events and you will feel a power guiding you beyond day-to-day struggles. If others are pulling you off balance, it is your responsibility to walk away, maintaining control at all times. It becomes doubly important to avoid confrontation because your life is like a stick floating down a river and interpersonal strife snags it, bringing your progress to a standstill. The old Taoist sages, who understood this flow of energy, taught their students to avoid confrontation, for it fuels the ego and strengthens the power of the subconscious over your affairs. The sage walks away, the fool stands and fights.

If someone wants something from you, give it to him or her. That is universal flow, for in doing so you are not holding on, your energy is fluid and it allows you to remain open to receive from other areas. If you are in an unbalanced relationship, fix it. If you cannot do so, leave. If you are hampered by a lack of money, put your trust in the Force and move toward your goals anyway. That is flow: being in balance with yourself allows the Force to work with you, all is maintained in your life, there will always be opportunities for growth, and people will seek you out.

Here is an exercise you might like to try. Rise at dawn and spend about an hour walking out of doors, silently reviewing any concerns you may have. Toward the end of the walk, select a large and powerful tree. Stand with your back to the tree, placing your hands behind your back against it. Take a deep breath and relax your entire body. Begin by acknowledging the spiritual evolution in nature. Take another deep breath and, while you exhale say, "May the Living Spirit grant evolution to the spirits of nature." Then take another deep breath and repeat your invocation for the spirits of fire, air, and water. In this way, you establish communication with your nature self and, if you are sensitive, you will feel the elements respond.

Next, feel the energy of the tree flowing down through its trunk into your body. As you begin this visualization, you may feel a slight rocking motion in your own energy. If you are sensitive, you will actually feel the power of the tree metaphysically cleaning your energy, for nature absorbs emotion. After a few moments, the movement will stop and you will not be able to absorb any more. Acknowledge the tree and the power of nature and realize that your power, in turn, helps the tree and nature to evolve, so there is a mutual exchange at a mystical level. Return home in silence.

Tension builds only when your mind has no release. By refreshing yourself through silence and nature, you constantly revitalize the *inner* you. Dawn is your strongest hour. If you can rise in time to meet the day, that effort becomes a discipline that you use to establish control. Take twenty-four minutes, one for each hour of the day, either meditating or walking in silence, but on your own. Use the time to project yourself into the day. As you center your mind, the power of your *Higher Self* goes out and surrounds the events you will meet, acting as a spiritual fore-runner, enlivening energy in front of you. Visualize your day flowing; see the people you will be dealing with responding to you positively; see your body strong and healthy; see the day in its creative splen-dor; see beauty in all things. Release any emotional problems from the previous day and take time to really feel the *inner* you. Say in your own words, "To-day is a beautiful day. I control what I am, and what I am has beauty and strength, and what I pull to me is for my highest evolution and good."

Finally, incorporate exercise into your daily regimen by including, say, twenty minutes of heart-pumping aerobic movement. This will help you to control your emotions, for exercise produces in the brain special chemicals called endorphins which naturally relax you.

By setting up your day before the rest of the world has risen, you establish an energy that cannot be overwhelmed by the negativity of others. When you use this technique, you will find that anger, judg-ment, and inter-personal squabbles fall away, as others get an inkling of your unseen power. The more you express this power, the more you will ex-perience an *inner knowing* that teaches you to evolve beyond the earth plane.

Leaving the earth plane and stepping into dimen-sions beyond the five senses without actually dying is accomplished through the fourth discipline, the discipline of balance. It allows you to live in the world without being a part of it, and sets you free to function at higher levels of perception, for the dimension in which you are heading is one of complete balance, and it will not open if what you are is falling apart.

Having created a discipline of physical, nutritional, and balanced emotional aspects, you will need fine-tuning. Meditating for twenty-four minutes a day gives you balance. Doing so for eight hours a day makes you unbalanced. Spiritual growth is not a matter of withdrawing from life, it is a matter of developing the power within you and then expressing it in some way. You are here to experience life, not to escape from it. It is useful to remember that energy must be delicately balanced and, as your energy rises and your perceptions grow, you will have to guard that fine line.

Everything that surrounds you has energy, being either alkaline, acid, or neutral. Your life should be like your food, about 80 percent alkaline. Of course, you will need a little acid for balance, but you get more than enough of that just walking down a city street or dealing with day-to-day thought forms.

Alkalinity surrounds you with a sympathetic energy, allowing the guide to communicate more freely and helping your body to heal itself. Look at your life and ensure that you have balance around you—not just in what you eat, but in the company you keep, the places you go, the colors and fabrics that surround you, the entertainment you enjoy, and the music you listen to. Each of these has alkaline/acid properties and it is simple to identify them.

Ask yourself is parsley alkaline or acid? Is coffee acid or alkaline? The answers come automatically. What about colors? Is red acid? Certainly, as are orange, yellow, and black. You should use those colors to accentuate, but they should not predominate in your home or in the clothes you wear. Red, orange, and yellow hold you into the physical, emotional, and mental energies and, by spiritually aligning with the Force, you are trying to go beyond these aspects. Black is the color of evolution, an imploding energy, not negative but basically an energy that is falling in on itself. The color is attractive to individuals who are involved in negativity and violence, because such people project fear, and black allows them to feel people's reactions, which gives them a feeling of power over others. The difficulty they eventually experience is that the negativity constantly coming back at them builds up until, one day, it is made manifest in some horrendous event. That is why many practitioners of black magic, unable to dissipate the energy they create, come to a grizzly end. The other main users of black are "ladies of the evening" who need to feel the sexual reactions of their clients; they wear black to allure. Black is neither good nor evil; it just implodes upon itself. Therefore, it should be used or worn sparingly.

Green is neutral and passive, the great relaxer. In the olden days, the area behind a theatrical stage was painted green in order to calm the actors before a performance. Nowadays, that area is sometimes known as "the green room" even when it is painted a different color. Green has the soothing effect of nature. Blue, indigo, and violet are alkaline, for they help you come in touch with your *Higher Self*. White is also alkaline and is a good color to wear if you deal with a lot of people; it protects you from their energy and reflects any negativity or imbalance that may be directed toward you. Most pastels are alkaline, because they are very soft and, even though they might tend toward physical, emotional, and mental colors, they express light and color with an understated beauty.

Fabrics are easy to discern. Cotton, wool, silk, and other natural fabrics are alkaline, whereas man-made fabrics such as polyester and rayon are acid; they retain a lot of static electricity and will gradually lower your energy in much the same way as neon lighting does.

There is also a balance in music. Rock an' roll—acid or alkaline? Debussy's *Clair de Lune*—alkaline or acid? It isn't difficult. Basically, rock, soul, and jazz are acid, whereas classical music is generally alkaline. Opera, on the other hand, varies; at times it is very acid and emotional and, at others, inspirational and alkaline, depending on the mood of the piece. What do you think Country and Western music might be? If you answer "acid," you are correct. Usually, the music is a story; the guy can't get his life together, his horse has died and his lady has taken her love to town—it is emotion, expressed as orange in the music and so an energy that will hold you in to the baser patterns. And that you have to watch. If you work in a place that constantly plays rock music, you will find it hard to stay balanced; the music will be continually pushing out its colors, red and orange, you will not be able to rest and, after a while, you will be unable to balance your inner strength.

Being sensitive to your surroundings helps you create a discipline of balance and whatever discipline you impose in dedication to your inner quest, strengthens you all the while. Of course, such dedication is not compulsory, but if you are serious about going beyond day-to-day reality, you will have to be sensitive to the world around you. If you are not sure whether or not a certain thing is helpful and alkaline, use this guideline: if it is physical, emotional, or mental, it is probably acid; if it is neutral, that is to say natural, or philosophical, or spiritual (not religious), it is alkaline and will help you to come in touch with yourself. By applying this rule of thumb, you establish the power to pull to you all that you will ever need, you will express the Force in such magnitude that you become an energy center unto yourself.

Then your creative abilities mingle with the Universal Law and life takes on a special spontaneity; money appears when you need it, people support what you are doing, and opportunities that will carry you to the next step crop up. Chance meetings, unusual happenings—through balance you become linked to the power of the universe and your possibilities expand to infinity.

Balance allows you to be unmoved by people, politics, supply, and demand: your energy exists apart from them and its spirituality gradually changes what you are. Through your intrinsic magnificence you pull to yourself automatically all that you need. The world's problems do not bring you down, for you are beyond them, observing life from the sidelines and, in so doing, you allow others their proper evolution—understanding all the while that, by being dedicated, you give strength inwardly to yourself and to the world around you. It is impossible to quantify your effect on others, but metaphysically your efforts contribute to the evolution of the world, for your energy is used by the higher powers to allow an inspiration to continue. The sage is never aware of how his power effects changes in others, and that is what makes him a sage.

Your power comes from understanding that where others are is where they need to be, and whatever they are doing is for their highest growth, and you should not judge it. By totally accepting other people's reality, you express true universal love and you invigorate your own progress, because judgment does not hold you back to the baser physical level.

Negativity, famine, pollution, nuclear bombs, interpersonal strife are all part of the curriculum of the physical experience—you will never change that, no one has. By being an observer, you rise above the quagmire of *karma* and this is what frees you to contribute through balance. It is an *inner* contribution that is little understood and receives no recognition, but the power is there and it creates opportunities, not only for yourself but for others. It is very special power, your gift, your discipline, your dedication to the Force.

Militancy is a trap. You cannot go beyond the world if you are angry with it. As your consciousness awakens, you might look around and say: "The world is a dreadful place. I'll have to fix this. Send some rice to the starving millions!" This is a natural reaction but it hides you from an infinite view of things. Do you think that the Force, the guides, and all the powers that oversee the earth plane could not change things in a second if they wanted to? Of course they could. But if they did, there would be no experience here, no challenge to step above. It would be like a tightrope-walker placing his rope on the ground. Who would pay to see that? Suffering is a part of each person's spiritual growth. You have been through it yourself, perhaps not in this lifetime, but in others. It is a valuable lesson and those experiencing the physical are graduating through it. It is impossible for us to judge accurately another's life, because we are not privy to all the circumstances that make up that person's inner being, and if we insist on interfering, then, someday, someone will interfere with our evolution.

How often have you begun a project only to have a well-wisher take the tools from your hands, and you wind up with a gate painted green when, in fact, you only wanted to change the hinge. That frustration is what is happening in a cosmic sense to the world today as well-wishers rearrange people's circumstances to fit their view of how things should be. If you want to change the world, change yourself, then others will be pulled to what you are, will change themselves, and all will come to a gradual understanding. For observation is power, judgment is weakness.

When you establish a discipline and maintain it for a while, the energy of your guide and of your *Higher Self* will really begin to flow—you will feel its presence. It will not be a voice from above but a communication from within. And it will be important for you to give credence to that communication. The difference between the sage and the ordinary man is that when the former receives a communication from within he acts, while the latter thinks it not true. Being in flow and a part of the Force will allow you to become sensitive to inner promptings. And though they may be just faint feelings, the more you acknowledge the communication the more the guide will convey.

One night, some years ago, as I lay on my bed after a very long day, an inner symbol appeared to me and said, "Rise from your bed and be at the waterfall in the mountains by midnight." I had an overwhelming reluctance to move. I was tired and the waterfall was forty miles away. I lay there tempted to ignore the whole thing but it seemed important and I forced myself to make the journey. The waterfall was a mile from the road and, as I climbed the mountain, my limbs ached and the howling of the mountain animals scared me. (Note: I say, "mountain animals." As a city person, I hadn't a clue what type of animals they were, but I know that when an animal howls it wants something and I had a feeling that I was the only "something" around those parts.) I tried moving faster, but in the darkness I constantly tripped and fell. I would gladly have lain there, had not fear and the cold of the night egged me on like a cosmic cattle prod.

I arrived at the waterfall five minutes before midnight and took a position on a flat slab beside the cascade. The experience was exhilarating and the moonlight bathed the whole scene in an eerie phosphorescence. As I sat and waited, I smiled at how much my life had changed in recent years. At the stroke of midnight, I felt an immense energy come around me, invisible but powerful. My respect for it seemed to hold me to the spot and, though I was overawed, I was not frightened, because somehow I knew the energy had my best interests at heart. It began by explaining the meaning of certain events in my life that had puzzled me for years and it gave me some predictions for the future. The process whereby the energy communicated was a high form of "thought transference," but its power was such that the message conveyed seemed inside me and outside at the same time. I was unable to discern whether it was a type of "strong inner talking," or whether I was listening to actual words. Momentarily I experienced being a part of all things. I and the energy were one and separate at the same time.

The energy gave me specific instructions and suggested I was to move to a nearby town, contact an old lady who lived there and make myself available to her in any way needed.

Driving back from the mountain, I pondered the significance of the old lady. But anyhow, the next day my wife and I moved to the nearby town and I made contact, as instructed. The old lady told me that she had been expecting me: she had just formed a small church and she wanted me to help her get it going. I agreed to be president and my wife played the organ. Neither of us had a clue what the church believed in but that did not matter, we were following instructions.

It took me two years to discover the significance of my association with the lady and her church. Through my link with her, my wife and I wound up in Europe, and there we accepted a metaphysical assignment that meant more to us than anything else we had ever experienced. If we had not moved to that small town and made the connection, we would have followed a different pattern and our destiny might still be floundering in an old energy.

It is important for you to believe what you hear and feel. Intuition is a great power, it is the *Higher Self* communicating, showing you which way to go. It is the voice that, as you enter the aircraft, says "sit there," and you find yourself next to the very connection you had been hoping to make for ten years. It is a power out ahead of you that will open doors and clear the path; but you have to do the walking, carry the load, so to speak. It is there, guiding you, and everyone has experienced it from time to time. As you open to the guide, you forge a permanent link, a connection that allows you sensory perception of other planes of existence.

That perception is not a voice from Heaven. It is an inner communication that is moving at a vibrancy much greater than you are used to. That is why you are not usually aware of its presence. Gradually, as your energy rises, you begin to hear, see, and feel the communication more strongly. It does not happen overnight, and your progress is predicated on how well you establish the four disciplines in your life.

Once you have mastered discipline and balance, you can familiarize yourself with the manner of communication. Since your whole life is a symbol, a synchronistic interplay of your inner energy, the communication can come from anywhere. As you raise your energy, the synchronization or the counterplay moves faster and faster and you automatically link your consciousness to all that is around you.

Twelve ducks flying upside down north to south mean nothing to the man in the street, but to you they might hold the answer to a monumental question. Some years ago I found myself in a complicated financial situation. I was faced with either accepting less than I wanted and leaving a specific area or holding out for more but having to stay and wait as the deal unraveled itself. I was walking on the beach, pondering the question, when I came across a child's playing card lying at my feet; picking it up I noticed it had an ordinary geometric pattern on one side while on the other it had the number eight. To my subconscious mind, the number eight represents the *ogdoad*, a symbol of money in Pythagorean numerology. Delighted with my find, I took the card to mean that I should accept the money and leave, which, as it turned out, was the right decision.

Now, people might say that it was just a coincidence and for some that would be true. But once in flow, you are inexorably linked to the whole cosmos and nothing is a coincidence, absolutely nothing. There are signs and lessons everywhere; in the things people say, in the circumstances that unfold through life, in the things you see as you move about.

The *Higher Self* is subtle. It does not bang you on the head with a plank. It allows gradual growth as you discover a deeper and deeper meaning to the world around you. Dimensions are inward; they unfold to energy like those Chinese dolls that you take apart to find another doll inside, and yet another and so on. Dimensions are infinite inner space, and the only thing that bars you from experiencing it all is incompatibility between your energy and the dimension you wish to experience. For dimensions permeate physical reality and, though you might not be aware of them, the sage standing next to you might.

Your mind is the block. It stands between you and the whole glory of the cosmic experience. However, it performs a vital function, for without the constraints of the mind and its physical housing, the brain, you would be overwhelmed by incoming sensory information. Your brain acts as an inhibitor, holding you in the physical plane long enough to experience it. When you come to the end of the earthplane cycle, your mind will be free of the brain and it will have less power to restrain you. You will discover your *Higher Self* and you will be off and running, so to speak. This power lies waiting for you and no matter at what stage you find yourself, sage or novice, there is more up ahead. If you are standing still thinking you have done enough, you obviously have not. Beware of teachers who say, "I have discovered the great cosmic way, follow me." For those who say they have, have not, and you cannot reach the dimension of your *Higher Self* by following a creed, an energy pattern created by the subconscious mind of another, no matter who. Right or wrong, you have to do it yourself: your life, your decisions, your experience of events.

There is a saying in Taoist philosophy which goes, "What is isn't, and what isn't is." This neatly summarizes the difference between being just in the physical world and believing that what you see is real, and being in the *illusion* of the *Higher Self* which is true reality. When you are in your *Higher Self*, you will find you can manipulate your own destiny, but you cannot reach that level of metaphysical ability by following someone else. You have to be out on your own, accepting your own promptings, your own inner messages, and you have to do this in silence. Often, those you leave behind will react. They will want you to endorse their viewpoint and support their system. But once you come into your *Higher Self* you develop a special independence. If you then resort to militancy, saying what you left behind is no good, society will string you up and you may find yourself experiencing your *Higher Self* from the next dimension, anyway.

We cannot go beyond the earth plane while criticizing it, for it serves us, as all restriction does. It holds us long enough for us to experience ourselves, whereby we understand the true nature of freedom. The system also serves those it holds today, for tomorrow they will step above it. To go beyond the earth plane you have to be able to accept it, to see beauty within it no matter what, to see it as perfect. Then you develop the spiritual maturity to leave things as they are, understanding that the Force knows what it is doing, and that pain, suffering, and the encasement of the physical are temporary conditions that people actually need for their spiritual growth.

Once you can step away and cease to judge others, allowing them to be without infringing on them or trying to save them (the last thing they need is someone to save them), you are ready through discipline to evolve from the physical. This process can be accomplished *before* you die and you literally perceive beyond the physical while still here. Death is not the only way out, but few people have discovered that for themselves. The ones who have are not around to talk about it.

When Lot's wife looked back at Sodom and Gomorrah and was turned into a pillar of salt, it signified metaphysically that, if you align with the carnal/physical, your energy becomes as coarse as that which surrounds you. To the writer of the story, a pillar of salt was about as physical as he could get, and so he said Lot's wife was turned into a pillar of salt, meaning her energy was so physical that she was not able to experience the higher spiritual planes that others in her group went on to. She was left behind.

This same situation is re-enacted the world over as each person chooses one path or another. A sojourn in Sodom and Gomorrah may be just what some people need, for perhaps cosmically they need to roll around in the physical, to taste it, to misuse it, to experience it falling apart on them. Once that is over, they are ready to accept a new experiment, a new attempt at balancing their energy.

It is all part of understanding the Force and how it works, and there is no better way than for the *Higher Self* to come down into the physical and find out. That is why what you are right now is so important. It is an experiment in higher energy and all the experiences you have ever had will be a part of your learning pattern that will not disappear at death but will be transmuted gradually so that you understand yourself in a more loving and magnanimous context.

That is also why, in the universal sense, there is no sin. When the *Higher Self* split itself into various experiences it knew there would be a possibility of infringement, restriction, strife, judgment, and so on. It accepted that, and viewed it as learning, as practice sessions for its energy. There is no punishment other than what you feel about your actions, and when you act contrary to the Universal Law you experience instant karma—energy coming back at you. It may not seem instant because of the slow vibrational field we are in, but in the cosmic sense it is immediate. In effect, your spirituality is measured by your capacity to be magnanimous, to open to all things, to truly express that limitless infinity within you.

CHAPTER 5: Love of the Force Sets You Free

As a small child, I was taught that God loved me. Then one day I fell out of a tree and I experienced pain. That pain persisted and for a while I could not understand why the Force had let me down. Each of us has gone through the same thing. As a child, I asked a clergyman what, in his opinion, was the answer to my dilemma, and I was disappointed that he had no good answer. He just mumbled something about God's plan.

Try explaining God's plan to a small boy who has just fallen from a tree. I remember thinking it all unfair, and I found the clergyman's explanation unsatisfactory. We are taught the Force loves us, and we then have to reconcile that with the mayhem around us. We watch while various religious groups battle each other in the name of God, each claiming the Force to his sole right, and we wonder what kind of God there must be out there who allows all this to happen.

The answer lies in a deeper understanding of the Force and the way energy flows. The Force loves you. But the concept was not properly understood by the philosophers who wrote the holy books, and that caused confusion. The love the Force has for you is not an emotional love that, say, a kindly uncle might have for his niece or a mother for her child. It is a love that comes from the fact that the Force loves *itself*. Therefore, because it is in you, it loves you, and the way to enhance that love is to love *yourself*. By doing so, you consciously concentrate on the Force and that makes it expand within you. This is not an egocentric, narcissistic love, but a love that comes from respecting all living things, and the greatest living thing under your immediate control is your own self.

Does this mean that you should not love others or go out of your way to help them? No. It means that you have to recognize yourself as God, as the infinite life force, and express that as strongly as you possibly can. Of course, charitable works have their place in the evolution of man but they do not greatly magnify the Force of those involved. If you send a bag of rice to a village in India, you have the emotional pleasure that doing so brings you and the villagers have the physical pleasure of eating the rice (if it ever gets there!) but neither of you has made much of an advance in perception of the Force. The Force, being beyond negativity, is not a part of the villagers' need, nor is it aware of your emotional pleasure. Through acts of kindness we practice magnanimity and the recipients feel that there is a power for good beyond their misery, but that is all. These actions rise and fall outside the Force's immediate perception; therefore they do not really expand an individual's expression.

Good works deal with external physical illusion rather than inner reality. That is why, if you concentrate on a God outside of yourself, you exert power in the wrong direction, and eventually it dissipates or weakens, rather than magnifies, what you are. By loving yourself and respecting all things, you complete an esoteric understanding of love which grants you added power and helps you to grow.

The part of your evolution that is the farthest to the outside of the *real* you is your physical body but, because you are in the physical, it dominates. By loving and caring for it, you are saying, "What I am is beautiful, what I am has value. I respect what I am, and I understand that each and every second of my life is an extension of the Force." Love of self and the respect that you show for your body is the first step in expanding your consciousness.

Most of the people who wake to a higher sense of consciousness do so through nutrition and health. They look at their bodies and they begin to feel that perhaps they can control their life and their experiences on the earth plane. This is the first step in understanding the love of the Force. It is why physical discipline is the first discipline of the initiates, not because anyone cares whether or not your body falls apart, but because concentrating on it and respecting it allows you to expand your *inner self.*

You respect your body by learning about it and taking care of it. The average man cares more for his possessions. He pollutes his body, abuses it, and eventually disease sets in. Worse than that, a lifetime passes without his ever having experienced a true heightened power of self. He perceives the world through a sluggish body, weak emotions, poor thinking, and he says, "This is the way it is." The initiate perceives the world from a position of power. He sees all the physical events but he also sees some of the non-physical happenings. His five senses expand to accept more information. Because his body is disciplined, its power oscillates faster than does the power of other bodies, and speed of oscillation is the initiate's secret: nothing more.

The unseen worlds of the initiates are right beside you, they permeate physical reality. As you grow to become a part of them, you will be surprised to find that they are not what you expected. This is because our current beliefs come out of the restrictions of the human mind. Once you cross over into the other worlds, you will find that the speed or quantity of the Force those dimensions express, grants them an electrifying spontaneity which makes our ordinary world seem sluggish. It is incumbent on you to raise your energy, for the heightened oscillation of the Force cannot come down for you. That is the beauty of the Force's impartiality and that is why the evolution of mankind, with all its ups and downs, is such a great awakening. It allows man eventually to understand that the only person who can help him is himself. Aid should be given in a way that allows the recipients to help themselves rather than as charity which, in effect, delays the day when they have the cosmic realization that they are the ones in charge.

Once you accept true spiritual responsibility, loving yourself comes easily, for you understand that it is you who control. If you lower your energy by, say, drinking too much, you cannot blame the Force for any imbalance you pull to you, because that imbalance is part of the energy pattern you have created.

When two cars collide, the event has a metaphysical energy pattern. Both drivers brought themselves to that point in time through their own expressions, feelings, and emotional balances or imbalances: the experience has a power. The collision, the injuries, the destruction have a vibrational oscillation, an actual metaphysical speed per millionth of a second.

The same applies to your body and your life. Its totality has a vibrational level that rises and falls according to your mood, your physical condition, and the extent to which you guard your energy. Let us say, hypothetically, the man in the street has an average vibrational scale of 18,000 to 24,000 vibrations per millionth of a second. When his energy is strong, his vibrational scale hovers around 24,000; when it is low, it might drop to 18,000 cycles.

Within that scale or band, there are millions and millions of probability patterns or events that have the same vibrational frequency. Positive, inspirational events will have a higher frequency than negative restrictive ones. So, a picnic in the country among friends and loved ones might have an average vibrational speed of, say, 24,000 cycles per microsecond. But if the picnic deteriorates into a violent family feud, then the overall energy of the people involved will suddenly drop down to, say, 18,000 cycles per micro-second.

The metaphysical energy of your life, constantly moves up and down within the wave band of energy you are able to maintain.

Therefore, if a car accident has a metaphysical vibrational speed of, say, 18,000 cycles per microsecond, and your energy moves up and down between 18,000 and 24,000 cycles, it follows that a car accident is a possibility in your destiny pattern. It is one of the things that can happen but as long as you keep your energy up, it never will.

Once you let your energy drop, your chance of misfortune rises dramatically. Of course, it is not a matter of luck but a matter of your energy being momentarily compatible with the energy of a car accident. Now, if you happen to be in a boat at sea, and your energy drops, your chances of a car accident are nil, but you may experience another low-energy event, as a shark nibbles your foot.

Energy has a spontaneity in the way it expresses

itself. So, it is difficult to say for certain that a person will definitely experience a particular event. But you can say that events in a certain range have a high probability pattern, because the person in question maintains a similar energy level.

Your life unfolds to the dictates of energy. Nothing less, nothing more. Once you come to grips with loving self and respecting the Force within you, the waveband of energy that is you moves faster and faster. If it goes beyond, say, 30,000 cycles per micro-second, the possibility of your being involved in any kind of accident becomes remote. Your energy enters a dimension of greater positivity. You will arrive at the crossroads ten minutes too late for there to be an accident, or something will cause you to take a different route. This is because your intrinsic spirituality or vibrational worth leads you away from negative events.

You might ask how can that be. It is a factor of energy as it seeks its own level. You cannot have two dissimilar energies oscillating side by side. If an energy of 18,000 cycles per micro-second tries to oscillate next to the energy of the initiate at, say, 100,000 cycles a micro-second, the slower energy tends to speed up for a bit but sooner or later it proves unable to keep up and falls away.

As you walk through life, you will interact and deal with many people who are operating at 18,000 cycles a micro-second and, while they will be exhilarated by your vibrational level, they will not follow you for long. As you say, "let us rise at dawn and swim in the lake and then we will have a nice green salad for breakfast," they will become distracted, make excuses, and you will hear the sound of footsteps gradually getting fainter. That is the way things should be. Each follows the path that is comfortable for him and we all have to experience fully the slower energy patterns before we can go beyond them.

Eventually, all come to understand how energy really works but thankfully no one is asking you to stick around and wait for the others, and that is also the way it should be. When your energy rises higher and higher and you find yourself in a vibrational scale of, say, 100,000 cycles per micro-second, although still on the earth plane, you go beyond it, and your energy is so fast that the casual observer just does not see you.

That is why you hear stories of initiates being able to appear and disappear at will. The observer does not see an initiate until the initiate, through an act of consciousness, concentrates on the observer. So an initiate at the crossroads would not be seen by the drivers in the accident. But if he then crossed the road to bandage their bodies, they would see him. Whatever you concentrate on as an act of mind is the dimension you are in. If you love your body and concentrate on the Force within, that very concentration pulls your energy gradually away from the earth plane. This is because you are going beyond the physical, emotional, and mental dimensions, beyond the ordinary man who fails to see beauty in all things, who does not accept responsibility for his life, who tends to blame others for his circumstances.

To expand your acceptance or love of the Force, you have to extend that love and respect to others. Respecting them in the spiritual sense means allowing each to have a spiritual fulfillment without you infringing upon their lives—in the same way as the guides and higher powers respected you and allowed you to pull yourself up from where you used to be. If the initiate at the crossroads ran out and tried to prevent the accident, he would infringe upon the drivers and would probably injure himself. So he stands to one side, the benign observer. Once the accident is over and the drivers have experienced a further part of their "growth process," the initiate steps forward and aids them as they cry for help. While he bandages their wounds, the drivers momentarily experience his higher energy pattern and little by little their perception grows. But if the initiate tried to force understanding on the drivers, he would only burn himself out and hinder his own.

The energy of detached observation is so powerful that if you couple it with non-judgment, you instantly enhance your own strength. But many people, especially those of us brought up in Western traditions, find it hard to do this because the whole Judeo-Christian ethic is centered on going out and converting others to the fold, feeding them, and enclosing them in structured belief patterns that act as a kind of spiritual scaffolding. This works well for souls who are in their early incarnations; it allows them time to understand themselves. That is why dogmatic religions do well in poor countries whose inhabitants are in their first few lifetimes on the earth plane and structure is just what they need. But when people eventually become more spiritually sophisticated, they incorporate different belief patterns that center on their spiritual individuality, away from churches, dogma, structure, and form. They need to experience freedom, for they are ready to leave the earth plane forever, they have gone beyond restriction. They are free.

Freedom was not the way of things two thousand years ago, when the Christian church was getting started. In its early years it came under great threat and for a while it looked as though it would completely die out—it badly needed supporters. The rulers and gentry of that time were either Romans or people financially influenced by Rome, and they tended to follow the Roman religion of Mythra and other cult religions. These leaders of society were not going to upset the status quo by siding with a radical new religion that would threaten their livelihood and position in Roman society. And so, generally speaking, the church had to search for members among the outcasts, the poor, and the lower classes. That is why the subject in the story of the Good Samaritan is a gentile, not a Jew or a Roman. What the church was saying was, it's O.K. if you are not one of the upper crust, the God Force is with you, it does not recognize rank or status, everyone is equal in the eyes of God. And that of course is true, for the Force cannot be higher than itself and, as it is in everyone, it makes us all equal.

In those days there was no advertising and little writing. The only way to promote beliefs was by word of mouth. It was hard work. You had to get people to attend meetings and you had to get them there during daylight hours, when most would be tending their flocks and doing whatever people did in biblical times. Promoters were faced with a double problem. They got around it cleverly by offering food as a way to get people to the meetings. People who were starving would have no time for philosophy, but once you fed them they tended to be more receptive. This worked well and the attendance figures proved it, so you have stories of the feeding of the five thousand, the loaves and the fishes, and so on. Once these techniques were refined, the promoters incorporated the giving of food, or charity, into the master plan, much in the same way a sales director today might give his sales people a structured merchandizing script and point-of-sales "freebies." The whole point is that it worked and was good for the church. And so you will find the giving of food, symbolically or literally, has been incorporated into many Christian ceremonies. Therefore, deep within our psyche is rooted the concept that we have a duty to gather the poor and the outcasts and feed them, even though the original intention was not for us to take on the burdens of the world but for the church to merchandize its meetings.

This does not mean you ignore the pleas of others. But there has to be a spiritual purity in the way you relate to the world. Everything you have and everything you are is on short-term rental from the Force. Therefore, if someone asks for something give it to them, otherwise you deny your ability to pull from the abundance around you. But to go out and infringe on people through haphazard charity is also a denial of the magnificence of the Force, for it does not allow them to experience the fullness of the Force for themselves.

Some of these concepts are hard to master at first, as they take you away from the norm, away from mass thinking, but spiritual growth always involves swimming against the tide. This is not a philosophy for everyone, it is a path of power for those who want to step beyond the physical to a totally different alignment. A Taoist sage watches the world with dispassionate calm. When a person performs good works he does not praise, when there is evil he does not condemn, for he allows each person to experience without infringement. Non-judgment is loving the Force within you by loving it in others and having the power to go beyond emotion by leaving each to his own.

You may consider that callous. Do we not have a duty to help others, to bandage their wounds, to send them food, and so on? If that is what you feel, then so be it. Within the Universal Mind there is no right or wrong. Charity deals only with the physical and, if you embroil yourself too deeply in the affairs of others, you condemn yourself to a probability pattern lower than your full potential. What is important is that you do not allow a misconceived idea of your obligations to hold you back. Many people fail to develop metaphysically because they put something else, be it church, state, or family, in front of their own development. In so doing they negate the Force within themselves, because what they are saying is, "I am worthless. This church, this state, this cause is more important than I." That is not your highest path.

You have infinite potential as your birthright and nothing should stand in your way. You are an individual. You have incarnated here to understand yourself, and a part of doing so is learning to relate to others, your family and loved ones, but eventually it comes down to you on your own. You do not have a responsibility for the growth of others. Your responsibility is to the Force within you, and you can never do more for the world than concentrate on that. Even though your contribution may not be obvious, on an inner level it becomes a great power.

When your expression of the Force is faster than that of another, his energy is increased by your presence. That is what was meant by the "grace of God"—the inner oscillation. It is power, and has a scale of force and even though we cannot measure it, it runs from high to low, and you can train yourself to be aware of it. Everyone you have ever dealt with, everyone you have walked past, has benefited from your energy, if that energy was high and in dedication to the purity of the Force. You will never know what your power did for others. You just express it strongly and it sustains and protects you. The dedication surrounds you with a mystique and that energy intermingles with others. This is your gift to mankind. People will send rice. You can be sure of that. But your gift is greater, silent, invisible. Rarely will anyone thank you, as we rarely thank the sun for shining upon us.

Non-judgment, therefore, is your affirmation that the world is beautiful, that all is growth and that you are going beyond it. Gradually, it disengages you from the earth plane and as you begin to leave, you find a need to resolve all inner conflicts, not only with self but with others. If you find you cannot resolve a situation with another individual, walk away, leave them to be what they are, which is after all perfect, given the time and place in their infinite evolution. The Universal Law is the Force in motion. It does not expect you to suffer a relationship that does not allow you growth. In fact, in a dispassionate way it wants you to have your freedom, for by unraveling the knots, you clear the way for more energy to flow from your *Higher Self*. Others are pulled by your intrinsic spiritual worth, not to what you say you are. By gradually developing non-judgment and non-conflict, you express the Force to its highest, and this helps you to grow.

As you begin the process of enhancing the Force within you, you have to consciously purify your energy at all times. This means taking care to release emotions, guarding against a build-up of negative energy, allowing your thought patterns gradually to strengthen as you concentrate on life. You may want to get out of your current circumstances and into others that will allow more balance. Do so. In the very change you will find creativity flows and the newness around you creates more opportunities. Many people sit around waiting for the world to discover them, and that rarely happens. If you move toward your goals, expressing all your power, opportunity will find you as a result of your actions. For by riding your energy, knowing and believing your *Higher Self* is with you, you will be in the right place at the right time. But make the first move, taking constant care to purify and review your life; move from negative habits into the fortress of light. Discipline is the horse you ride.

The Force is there, ready and waiting, neutral. If you are prepared to accept a higher power, you will step into an extraordinary state of consciousness, and that you will find challenging, for it lies always beyond where you are now, moving ever faster and faster.

CHAPTER 6: Your Life's Ultimate Goal

Let us review: you are not your physical body, your emotions, or your intellect. You are the infinite, limitless energy of your *Higher Self* experiencing for a short while here on earth evolution *within* your body. The Force and you are one and the same, and the more you align with the positive, limitless, pure you, the more of the Force you express. By developing its energy within you, you can learn to communicate with an infinite source of knowledge. This allows an acceleration of spiritual growth, for you have access to information not only from the past but from the present and the future. That knowledge is waiting for you to make use of it, and personal balance is the key to its access. Through balance, you open within yourself a door that allows perception of other worlds, and that perception is vital to your journey or quest.

Before incarnating in your physical body, your *Higher Self* had an opportunity to survey the situation it was about to enter, and accepted the circumstances of your life as a part of its heroic goal. It knew that if it could succeed in this existence, it would be able to go on to an even greater expression of the Force.

Attached to your *Higher Self* is an energy whose responsibility it is to assist you in your evolution. We call that energy *the guide*. It is a spirit entity that has completed all its lives as a human on the earth and is now experiencing spiritual evolution as a helper, pushing energy through into the physical plane. Since its progress is inexorably linked to yours, the guide has an interest in making sure you do well. Often, the guide is someone with whom you have had a past life, who is familiar with your energy and its needs. The function of the guide is to project energy or inspiration to allow you the maximum unfolding in this existence, so that you attain your life's heroic goal.

That goal is known only to you, your guide, and your *Higher Self.* If you are young, it probably lies ahead of you; if you are old, you have probably gone through a good part of it, but there is always time to fine-tune what you are; to pull it all together into one crescendo of energy until, finally, you leave the earth forever, to experience heightened forms of existence in other dimensions.

How do you discover the nature of your life's goal? Usually, it is a matter of resolving something within yourself, rather than a mission to save the world. It consists of confronting and going beyond the very thing that you find the hardest to face or deal with. It could be trials and tribulations over money, or a problem with love of self, or, through various incarnations, you might have failed to come into a natural understanding of sexuality and are here this time to experience physicalness, motherhood perhaps, or dealing successfully with your body, away from misuse and, possibly, guilt.

Sometimes, your life's goal involves another person. Maybe you are here to resolve a conflict with someone that has gone on through many lifetimes. Now, you and that person find yourselves mother and son, brother and sister, or husband and wife. This time you are here to deal equably with that person and your other family members, remembering all the while that, once you elevate yourself metaphysically, you are no longer allowed to infringe on others. You should allow each to develop at his or her own speed and to make his or her own decisions.

If you find yourself in a difficult relationship with someone, you can be sure that that very situation is a part of your life's goal; you have to learn to deal with it fairly and lovingly, resolving conflicts as best you can, allowing that person his or her highest growth without holding yourself back. Perhaps you find yourself in the burdensome situation of being custodian of someone who is mentally deficient, or of a spirit evolving in an imperfect body that needs your care, or perhaps of a family member in need of financial support. Helping that person will probably be a major part of your life's goal. There will be a spiritual reason why you find yourself in this position and, by accepting it and working through it in love and service, the situation will change somehow and, transcending your difficulties, you will step to freedom. You will stand in the complete glory of your inner self, a spirit, a power, ready to move on, ready to accept a new and brighter assignment.

Some people's life goal is to express a creative endeavor, which might be in the fine arts, in business, on the land, or in any other capacity where you challenge yourself creatively. You are here to learn to develop your inner creative energy to its highest without causing imbalance. Therefore, you begin to paint or write or compose or express yourself in some way but, as you do so, you make sure that you have your life in reasonable order. It is pointless to be the "grand master" if you die of drink at the age of thirty-three and cause financial havoc all around you.

You have to temper your creativity by balancing the other areas of your life, not infringing on others or forcing them to make up for your inability to handle the simple things, such as paying the rent. If your creativity does not support you at this time, reduce your obligations to bare minimum and mix your creativity with another endeavor that will allow you financial stability while you perfect your craft and gain acceptance.

The life goal of many involves dealing with their body. They either create or inherit an imperfection which they learn to deal with. If you are such a person, the very thing in your body that causes so much trouble is the weak spot in the spiritual you. By identifying and controlling it, you go beyond it, for it forces you to concentrate on yourself. In doing so, you look and wonder and, through wondering, you learn to understand energy and you see that its misuse creates imbalances, and understanding that helps you evolve beyond the earth plane.

Weakness in your spiritual self often manifests itself as various forms of emotional energy, which eventually show up in your body as physical problems. By looking at your body, you can learn about your inner self. It is a bit like translating a book from Hebrew into Greek, then into Latin, and finally into English. It loses a little in the telling, but you get the gist of it. By working on your physical self, you begin to face the emotional problems that cause your body to become ill at ease, and gradually you patch up and strengthen your spiritual self also.

Once you complete that, you are either healed or you leave the earth plane, but you do so as a complete entity, a spiritual power that can be used for the benefit of the universe at large by assisting others to evolve. No one can really explain the miracle of self that awaits you. You have to experience it through your own efforts. Whatever you set out to do in dedication and love of self is instantly rewarded on an inner plane, and you experience that reward in this life and in the afterlife.

To establish strong spiritual growth, you have to be in control of your mind. Otherwise, its reasonableness will trick you into accepting less than the best. It does so to avoid facing your life's heroic goal, which it finds uncomfortable. By its nature it will constantly pull you down an undisciplined path because it knows that, when you wallow in weakness, it is in control.

Your goal, therefore, is to concentrate on your strengths, believing in yourself, loving yourself, not infringing on others and going beyond those things that you find the hardest to deal with. Accepting that goal is half the battle, taking responsibility for yourself is the other half. When you can stand with your life firmly in your hands and say, "Force, guides, *Higher Self,* I take full command of my life and I am working on the bits I don't like," you come into cosmic maturity; events around you become a symbol of what you are and the Force supports you because you are not leaning on others metaphysically. Through this simple dedication you enter an elite group. Once you have cleared out the debris that has accumulated over the years, you will be able to develop the power of the Force in the New World, the one that is being gradually created by the few who know where the destiny of man really lies.

What, therefore, is your gift to humanity? It is to express what you are in beauty and strength, knowing that you are an eternal power. A sparrow has beauty because it expresses the Force naturally. It is its very essence, or its birdlikeness, that gives it charm, and yet what does it amount to? A sparrow is no more than a little lump of bone and feather, two toothpicks for legs, and a silly "tweet" for a voice, but it gives pleasure without even knowing it. The reason for this is that its power is not cluttered by mind or emotion. It is pure, a spontaneous example of the life force in motion.

Imagine what potential to express the Force you would have if you could reach the uncluttered purity of a small bird. What would be your power to give pleasure and inspiration? It would be immense, would it not? Through your efforts, others would rebuild themselves for they would see that, within the turmoil and chaos, there was a bird singing, there was a power, a pathway out of the morass. They would be able to see you just a way down the path ahead of them, and they would say if he or she can make it, so can I.

That is your gift. The pure self you express: your smile, the way you walk, the things you do, the way you drive your car, the way you handle your children, your daily dedication to those around you. That is your gift. As you develop yourself spiritually, people will come to you, for the Force knows how to make use of its supporters and it will allow you, through the intrinsic value of your spiritual energy, to go further, to shine ever more brightly. And you will understand more and more deeply that what you are is God.

There is nothing that you cannot do. There are no real limits to your capacity. Your heritage is to express a power for the benefit of yourself and then of others, and, by silently expressing that power, you allow a renaissance to come about.

Within mankind, there is a long-forgotten dream. It

is a dream of a time when purity of spirit ruled the earth, when love truly supported mankind, when each had time to evolve as he or she wished, a time when the individuality of self was revered; a time when there were no governments, no religions, no rules or regulations, for each person understood his responsibility to others and there was no infringement or mass thinking or forced conformity. There was spontaneous enlightenment, instinctive creativity, and you heard the laughter of man having fun.

Through your knowledge and power, that time will return. Not for all mankind, but for you and those who will be attracted to individuals such as you, who are expressing powerfully. For, in the darkest times, the Force always provides a spark of light and that light is carried by a few and later passes to others.

Your heritage, your life's heroic goal, is to work upon yourself to the point where the Force grants you the right to carry its light. And when you have done so for a while, you will earn the right to go to other things. You will look back at the world and you will hear a funny bag of bones with toothpick legs go "tweet" and somewhere a man will laugh in an atmosphere of total calm and you will be able to say to yourself, "I helped create that."

And you will know what is meant by the "Golden Age."

ABOUT THE AUTHOR

Lecturer and author Stuart Wilde is considered one of the most dynamic personalities in the Human Potential Movement today. He has appeared on over four hundred television and radio shows in nine countries, and he numbers his worldwide audience at over ten million.

Born in Farnham, England, the son of a British diplomat, Stuart Wilde became comfortable with many different cultures at an early age. After a twelve-year training in the esoteric traditions of ancient European and Eastern mysticism, Stuart traveled the equivalent of eighty times around the world in his personal metaphysical quest for knowledge.

From that rich experience he offers us the Warrior's Wisdom, a practical, "alternative" philosophy which gives power back to the individual. His charismatic style is unique among modern teachers, for he comes from a place of love in which he asks nothing of you other than that you feel good about yourself. He does not preach, solicit donations or manipulate the individual into a "group reality".

Stuart Wilde's mode of presentation allows you to feel safe. Using his rare brand of English humor, he presents complex information in a language everyone can understand. There is something different about Stuart. You won't be able to quite put your finger on it, but simply standing in his presence can cause your life to change in miraculous ways.

Stuart Wilde's creativity is prolific. He has recorded literally hundreds of teaching tapes, in both audio and video format, which are distributed in twenty-four countries around the world.

His eight books; *Miracles, The Force, Affirmations, Life Was Never Meant to be a Struggle, The Quickening, Trick to Money is Having Some, Secrets of Life*, and *Whispering Winds of Change* are considered masterpieces in their category and are currently being translated into all major European languages. In addition, he sits on the board of over a dozen international organizations which promote world understanding, abundance and the sanctity of the individual.

THE WARRIOR'S WISDOM BY STUART WILDE

Come to the cliff, he said.
They said, we are afraid.
Come to the cliff, he said.
They came.
He pushed them.
And they flew.

The **Warrior's Wisdom** is a four-day intensive. For an **information pack** on the **Warrior's Wisdom**, including full-color poster and cassette tape, **and other Stuart Wilde Seminars**, send $5 (p&h) to:

White Dove International
P.O. Box 1000
Taos, NM 87571
Phone (505)758-0500
Fax (505)758-2265

Consolidate your personal power through etheric strengthening and the positive occult perceptions of the Warrior-Sage.

BOOKS BY STUART WILDE

THE QUICKENING

ISBN 0-930603-22-2   **$9.95**

The Quickening discusses the power of the ancient Warrior-Sages and it teaches the reader etheric (Life Force) and psychological techniques for consolidating his or her energy for that final push to the peak within the Self.

AFFIRMATIONS
ISBN 0-930603-36-2   **$9.95**

This book, *Affirmations*, serves not so much to give you nice words to say to yourself, but as a magnificent and devastating battleplan, where you learn to expand the power you already have in order to win back absolute control of your life.

THE FORCE
ISBN 0-930603-00-1   **$7.95**

The Force, like your Higher Self, is an energy that experiences evolution. It is massive, exhilarating, magnanimous beyond description~perhaps you might want to call it God. It is growing, dynamic and has an inner drive or desire to become more of itself...everything has the Force within.

MIRACLES
ISBN 0-930603-01-X   **$4.50**

To create miracles, you have to be very clear about what it is you want. By being forthright and acting as if you have already obtained the object or condition that you desire, you create such a powerful energy that the Universal Law gives you what you want.

Please ask for Stuart Wilde's books and tapes at your local book store. Should you have any difficulty, contact White Dove to order by mail or by phone, and for the latest Stuart Wilde catalogue. White Dove, P.O. Box 1000, Taos, NM USA 87571, Phone 505-758-0500, Fax 505-758-2265

BOOKS BY STUART WILDE

LIFE WAS NEVER MEANT TO BE A STRUGGLE
ISBN 0-930603-04-4 $1.95

This amusing little book helps you identify the cause of struggle in your life and shows how to eliminate it quickly, through a concerted action plan. Your heritage is to be free. To achieve that you have to move gradually from struggle into free FLOW.

THE TRICK TO MONEY IS HAVING SOME
ISBN 0-930603-48-6 $10.95

Stuart Wilde's money book, deals with the e.s.p. of easy money and the metaphysics of being in the right place at the right time, with the right idea and the right attitude. Like his other highly successful books, this work is chock full of useful information. His breezy and comical style make for effortless reading, as you plot your path to complete financial freedom.

THE SECRETS OF LIFE
ISBN 0-930603-03-6 $9.95

The Secrets of Life is a collection of excerpts and quotes They form the basis of Stuart Wilde's "alternative philosophy" which has attracted such a large readership over the years.

WHISPERING WINDS OF CHANGE
ISBN 0-930603-45-1 $10.95

Stuart Wilde's latest book.

VIDEOS FROM STUART WILDE

In Search of the Super Self
ISBN 0-930603-38-9 Single Video 76 Min. $34.95

This original and fast-moving video seminar gives you practical, esoteric techniques for thought-form empowerment. The difference between success and failure is often very little. Learn how subtle energies affect your life. Be aware that even a small shift in your metaphysical understanding can bring you almost instant rewards. Harness the power of your Life Force by identifying with it and develop a congruence with your infinite power that is almost unstoppable. By detaching from your weaknesses and concentrating all your energies on your heroic quest in life, that super-self within you moves from imagination into reality. Step up and enjoy!

Mastery of Money
ISBN 0-930603-37-0 Single Video 71 Min. $34.95

In this entertaining video seminar, lecturer-author Stuart Wilde talks about money as energy. It is a vital part of your spiritual quest, for you need money to buy life's experiences. Once you can see money as energy there is no limit to how much money you can acquire. Stuart's highly successful metaphysical approach shows you how to get into the flow of "easy-money". He discusses practical techniques on how to raise your energy quickly. Once you do, people will be naturally attracted to what you are. When they show up, bill'em.

Soul Mates
ISBN 0-930603-27-3 Single Video 100 Min. $34.95

In this delightful seminar, Stuart Wilde addresses the modern day problem of interpersonal relationships. He shows you in practical day-to-day terms how to create a powerful energy within you so that the soul mate you have or the one you pull to you will allow you to participate in an intimate and exciting expression of human relations. Learn an understanding of esoteric sexuality and use that energy to heal your life and pull from the inner resources of Life Force that exist everywhere.

SUBLIMINAL TAPES FROM STUART WILDE

The subliminal affirmations on these tapes are embedded in a musical background. Your conscious mind hears only the music while your subconscious mind, your motivating force, accepts the powerful affirmations. There is no talking or introduction to these tapes-just a full hour of energy-creating messages laid under inspirational new age music.

All Subliminals are Single Cassettes at $11.95

ABUNDANCE
A Sack of Polished Emeralds
ISBN 0-930603-28-1
Abundance is so much a matter of how you feel. In order for you to pull more money into your life both your intellect and the *inner you* have to agree to accept more abundance.

CREATIVITY
Manifesting Your Creativity
ISBN 0-930603-40-0
Pure creativity is not learned. It is a matter of having the courage to develop it from within you and committing to a belief in yourself. Reprogram your mind with this subliminal tape to manifest the tangible successes that your creative splendor deserves.

COURAGE
I Can Do Anything
ISBN 0-930603-49-4
Fly like an eagle to the upper limits of your life! Dare to believe in your own power and watch the magic happen! Use this excellent tape to help you listen to your heart and to channel the rivers of power and energy already within you to make your dreams come true. There is no limit to what you can do.

DEEP SLEEP
ISBN 0-930603-29-X
This tape, with its peaceful affirmations, will help you get the rest you need. It also works while you are asleep, reinforcing the idea that you are in control of your sleeping patterns. It will help you be more receptive to your other subliminal programs. The affirmations are embedded in a soothing background of new age music with no talking or introduction.

ENERGY
I Am Power
ISBN 0-930603-07-9
This High Energy subliminal tape, written and produced by Stuart Wilde, is especially designed to quickly create energy for you when needed.

FEMININITY
Feminine Spirituality
ISBN 0-930603043-5
A woman's true warrior power lies deep within her. This subliminal tape reprograms your mind to remember that! The natural power and beauty within you is limitless. Realign and heal with the spiritual energy of Mother Earth.

MORE LOVE
Tender Moments
ISBN 0-930603-21-4
This subliminal tape is especially designed to assist in opening yourself to receive and give more love. The subliminal affirmations are to help you pull that "special" person into your life or develop a greater sense of love and caring for those who are already around you.

OPPORTUNITIES
Pulling Opportunities Like Plums From A Tree
ISBN 0-930603-09-5
This subliminal tape is especially designed to pull opportunities to you by programming your mind to the possibility of new and exciting change.

SUBLIMINAL TAPES FROM STUART WILDE

RELEASING
Waving Good-bye, Leaving and Smiling
ISBN 0-930603-42-7
Releasing situations can be hard because the mind tends to hold on. Use this tape to get over the people, places, jobs and old energies that you feel you need to "step beyond." Give the past "the boot." Step into a new, happier and more prosperous life.

QUIT SMOKING
Release Smoking Forever
ISBN 0-930603-32-X
To release smoking forever takes effort and courage. These subliminal affirmations will help you create a powerful *inner* feeling that you are in fact a non-smoker and that you can release smoking forever.

SPIRITUAL HEALING
Healing Rays From A Higher Power
ISBN 0-930603-08-7
To heal your body your mind has to be inspired to do so. On this subliminal tape we call upon that Higher Power within us to grant us the energy we need to realign our body.

STRESS REDUCTION
ISBN 0-930603-39-7
Our bodies are naturally designed to cope with stress. However, in the hectic pace of the modern day we can become overwhelmed by the complexities of life. Use this tape to re-establish the natural balance inherent in mind, body and spirit.

WEIGHT LOSS
I Feel Thin
ISBN 0-930603-10-9
Dieting and looking good do not have to be a struggle with this very effective subliminal weight loss program. Reprogram your mind to lose weight effortlessly by listening to subliminal affirmations embedded in a musical background.

MASCULINITY
ISBN 0-930603-52-4
The spiritual male is confident of his sexuality and sensitive to the needs of others. He knows that his ability to be magnanimous is the touchstone of his spiritual growth. He aligns with his power and pulls to himself what he needs to meet his obligations as the "out-going" creator of the earth plane.

WILDE CARDS
Retail Price $1.95 each
Twenty-four of Stuart Wilde's personal favorite affirmations are now available as individual magnetic cards. These eye-catching, metallic-colored WILDE CARDS can be displayed in a prominent place in your daily life to help reaffirm these positive messages from the Wilde Man.

If your local bookstore does not carry the tapes listed, have them contact the publisher for a list of distributors. They may write to **White Dove International, Inc., P.O. Box 1000, Taos, NM 87571 USA** or call **505-758-0500, Fax 505-758-2265**

SELF-HELP TAPES FROM STUART WILDE

AFFIRMATIONS
ISBN 0-930603-15-X
Two-Tape Series $21.95
Most of the organizations and structures in the world are designed to take away your power. This highly successful two-tape series serves not as a way to give you nice words to say to yourself but rather as a magnificent battleplan whereby you learn to expand the power you already have in order to win back absolute control over your life.

ANCIENT WISDOMS
The Path Of The Unknown Sages
ISBN 0-930603-33-8
Single Cassette $9.95
In this tape Stuart Wilde discusses the evolution of mankind through the great civilizations of Egypt, Lemuria and China and talks of cataclysms that have heralded new evolutions for the earth plane. Side two deals with Taoist philosophy and the esoteric concepts of *unknown sages*.

ASSERTIVENESS
Gettin' What You Want
ISBN 0-930603-41-9
Two-Tape Series $21.95
Learn how to hone your will so that life gives you what you want, with no other excuse, reason, or apology other than that you demand it.

CAMELOT
Its Power to the Present Day
ISBN 0-930603-16-8 $21.95
The legend of Camelot and the quest for the Holy Grail has fired the imagination of poets, artists and visionaries for generation upon generation. The power of *quest* is still alive for us today, because it places responsibility for our enlightenment and growth where it belongs--within ourselves. Used properly, the power of *quest* brings your life and the light within you to its highest possible expansion.

DEVELOPING THE SIXTH SENSE
ISBN 0-930603-11-7
Four-Tape Series $29.95
We are all special beings who possess an ability to perceive beyond the physical plane. Too often, through lack of direction or perhaps lack of commitment, people fail to achieve mastery of that elusive extrasensory power that is really a part of every individual's potential.

FREEDOM
Expanding Personal Freedom
ISBN 0-930603-23-0
Two-Tape Series $21.95
Stuart at his very best teaches that the only way to reach fulfillment and absolute safety in the coming years is to completely detach from the weakness inherent in the aspirations of man and to develop a vice-like grip on your own self-improvement. If you are ready, and you are dedicated to yourself, this tape is for you.

HIGHER SELF
Aligning To Your Higher Self
ISBN 0-930603-24-9
Single Cassette $9.95
The Higher Self is a collective body of energy-it is the *inner* you. Within it is all the knowledge that you will ever need and through it you can experience a limitless understanding of the physical plane as well as the "unseen dimensions" that lie close at hand.

JOY
Falling In Love With Life
ISBN 0-930603-46-X
Single Cassette $11.95
SIDE A- Stuart Wilde reminds you to celebrate life no matter what. He gives you practical techniques for re-establishing and sustaining joy and exhilaration in your heart. A nice gift for a friend. SIDE B-A subliminal tape crammed full of positive affirmations to lift your spirits.

SELF-HELP TAPES FROM STUART WILDE

THE MASTERY OF MONEY
ISBN 0-930603-14-1
Four-Tape Series $29.95
The Mastery of Money series is one of our very best sellers. Recorded live in Melbourne, Australia, this series looks at practical and esoteric techniques for *consciousness alignment* that allow you to step effortlessly into abundance.

MEDITATION
On The Edge
ISBN 0-930603-26-5
Two-Tape Series $21.95
Side one of this two-tape series discusses how to get real value from your meditations and gives you techniques for expanding contact with the inner worlds and your Higher Self. Sides two, three and four are unusual guided meditations centering on Pulling Instant Power, Spiritual Healing, and Contacting the Reservoirs of Talent Deep Within.

THE MIND
The Power Of The Subconscious Mind
ISBN 0-930603-44-3
Single Cassette $9.95
So much of your personal power lies dormant in the inner mind waiting for you to reclaim it. Listen to author Stuart Wilde talk to you about unleashing the awesome power of the shamanistic mind. Use the practical techniques he offers to whip-saw life into giving you what you want.

THIRTY-THREE STEPS BEYOND THE EARTH PLANE
ISBN 0-930603-19-2
Eight-Tape Series $69.95
Many consider the *Thirty-Three Steps* to be Stuart Wilde's definitive work. The quality of the series and the catchy title have insured its popularity. The material discusses thirty-three ancient wisdoms drawn from the Tao and the teachings of the initiates of bygone ages.

TRANCE STATES
And Theta Brain Waves
ISBN 0-930603-20-6
Two-Tape Series $21.95
The theta dimension is a source of inspiration and learning and it will bring you deeply in touch with your *inner guidance*. The first three sides of this series discuss the benefits of theta states. The fourth side is the theta metronome sound and a meditation exercise which will help you achieve theta effortlessly in your own meditation.

THE SUBTLE ART OF NEGOTIATING
ISBN 0-930603-55-9
Two-Tape Series $21.95
Everything is negotiable. PROFIT, according to Stuart Wilde, is an acronym for the components of a strong negotiating position. Combine these components with an understanding of the subtle art of negotiating and you will place yourself powerfully on the high ground in all of you business and personal dealings.

DREAM POWER
ISBN 0-930603-54-0
Two-Tape Series $21.95
We spend a third of our lives asleep, much of it dreaming. As a first step to better understanding your life and the relationships you are involved in, Stuart explains how to interpret and harness the power of your dreams.

DEVELOPING MORE SELF-CONFIDENCE
ISBN 0-930603-53-2
Two-tape Series $21.95
Stuart shows you how to arrange your thinking to develop a sense of positive expectancy. Learn how to dominate the reality around you so the circumstances of your life become an affirmation of your ever-expanding self-confidence.